I0415657

Campsite Impact in the Wilderness of Sequoia and Kings Canyon National Parks

Thirty Years of Change

Natural Resource Technical Report NPS/SEKI/NRTR—2013/665

David N. Cole and David J. Parsons

Aldo Leopold Wilderness Research Institute
USDA Forest Service
Rocky Mountain Research Station
790 East Beckwith Avenue
Missoula, Montana 59801

January 2013

U.S. Department of the Interior
National Park Service
Natural Resource Stewardship and Science
Fort Collins, Colorado

The National Park Service, Natural Resource Stewardship and Science office in Fort Collins, Colorado, publishes a range of reports that address natural resource topics. These reports are of interest and applicability to a broad audience in the National Park Service and others in natural resource management, including scientists, conservation and environmental constituencies, and the public.

The Natural Resource Technical Report Series is used to disseminate results of scientific studies in the physical, biological, and social sciences for both the advancement of science and the achievement of the National Park Service mission. The series provides contributors with a forum for displaying comprehensive data that are often deleted from journals because of page limitations.

All manuscripts in the series receive the appropriate level of peer review to ensure that the information is scientifically credible, technically accurate, appropriately written for the intended audience, and designed and published in a professional manner. This report received informal peer review by subject-matter experts who were not directly involved in the collection, analysis, or reporting of the data.

Views, statements, findings, conclusions, recommendations, and data in this report do not necessarily reflect views and policies of the National Park Service, U.S. Department of the Interior. Mention of trade names or commercial products does not constitute endorsement or recommendation for use by the U.S. Government.

This report is available from the Sequoia and Kings Canyon National Parks website (http://www.nps.gov/seki/index.htm) and the Natural Resource Publications Management website (http://www.nature.nps.gov/publications/nrpm/).

Please cite this publication as:

Cole, D. N. and D. J. Parsons. 2013. Campsite impact in the wilderness of Sequoia and Kings Canyon National Parks: Thirty years of change. Natural Resource Technical Report NPS/SEKI/NRTR—2013/665. National Park Service, Fort Collins, Colorado.

NPS 102/119561, January 2013

Contents

Page

Figures.. iv

Tables viii

Appendices ix

Executive Summary xi

Acknowledgments xiii

Introduction 1

Study Area 3

    Visitor Use 3

    Visitor Use Management 7

Methods 9

    The Initial Survey, 1976-1981 9

    The Repeat Survey, 2006-2007 13

    Field Trips and Interviews 16

    Data Analysis 16

Results 19

    Campsite Conditions in 2006-2007 19

        Number and Condition of Campsites 21

        Variation in Campsite Number and Condition 22

    Change in Campsite Conditions since the 1970s 31

        Variation in Campsite Number and Condition 34

        Why Some Subzones Improved More Than Others 41

Study Limitations 45

Discussion and Management Implications 47

Contents (continued)

Page

Why Have Conditions Improved So Much?..48

   Amount of Use..48

   Distribution of Use...49

   Visitor Behavior...50

   Campsite Management Implemented By Wilderness Rangers...........................51

   Recommendations...52

Conclusion 55

Literature Cited 57

iv

Figures

Page

Figure 1. Trends in wilderness use, as reported on wilderness permits. 4

Figure 2. Map of Sequoia and Kings Canyon National Parks showing the subzones
that were inventoried in 2006-2007 15

Figure 3. Class 1 site that is barely noticeable. 20

Figure 4. Class1 site with vegetation loss and a firepit. 20

Figure 5. Class 2 site with a substantial central area lacking vegetation. 20

Figure 6. Class 3 site without vegetation, litter or duff. 20

Figure 7. Class 4 site with widespread severe impact. 20

Figure 8. Variation in campsite impact with distance from water, 2006-2007 (mean
weighted value and standard error). 22

Figure 9. Differences in campsite impact between overstory types, 2006-2007 (mean
weighted value and standard error). 23

Figure 10. Differences in campsite impact between forest overstory cover classes,
2006-2007 (mean weighted value and standard error). 24

Figure 11. Differences in campsite impact between understory types, 2006-2007
(mean weighted value and standard error). 24

Figure 12. Variation in campsite impact with distance from food storage lockers,
2006-2007 (mean weighted value and standard error). 26

Figure 13. Variation in campsite impact with firewood availability, 2006-2007 (mean
weighted value and standard error). 27

Figure 14. Variation in campsite impact with evidence of stock impact, 2006-2007
(mean weighted value and standard error). 28

Figure 15. Variation in campsite impact with elevation zone, 2006-2007 (mean
weighted value per subzone campable mile and standard error). 28

Figure 16. Variation in campsite impact with distance from the closest trailhead,
2006-2007 (mean weighted value per subzone campable mile and standard error). 29

Figure 17. Variation in campsite impact with distance from the closest ranger station,
2006-2007 (mean weighted value per subzone campable mile and standard error). 29

Figures (continued)

Page

Figure 18. Variation in campsite impact with primary type of trail access, 2006-2007 (mean weighted value per subzone campable mile and standard error). 30

Figure 19. Variation in campsite impact with level of overnight stock use, 2006-2007 (mean weighted value per subzone campable mile and standard error). 30

Figure 20. Variation in campsite impact with whether campfires are prohibited or allowed, 2006-2007 (mean weighted value per subzone campable mile and standard error). 31

Figure 21. Change in number of sites impacted by camping, by condition class, between 1976-1981 and 2006-2007. 32

Figure 22. Change in number of sites impacted by camping, by condition class, between 1976-1981 and 2006-2007, assuming that 80% of restoration sites were class 1 sites and the rest were class 2 sites. 33

Figure 23. Change in number of campsites between 1976-1981 and 2006-2007, with distance of campsite from water. Numbers above bars are the percent change. 34

Figure 24. Change in number of sites impacted by camping and weighted value per campable mile, between 1976-1981 and 2006-2007, by elevation zone 35

Figure 25. Change in number of sites impacted by camping between 1976-1981 and 2006-2007, by forest overstory type 36

Figure 26. Change in weighted value per campable mile for all sites impacted by camping, between 1976-1981 and 2006-2007, by forest overstory type 36

Figure 27. Change in number of sites impacted by camping and weighted value per campable mile, between 1976-1981 and 2006-2007, by distance from the closest trailhead. 37

Figure 28. Change in number of sites impacted by camping and weighted value per campable mile, between 1976-1981 and 2006-2007, by distance from the closest ranger station 37

Figure 29. Change in number of sites impacted by camping and weighted value per campable mile, between 1976-1981 and 2006-2007, by type of trail access.. 39

Figure 30. Change in number of sites impacted by camping and weighted value per campable mile, between 1976-1981 and 2006-2007, by amount of overnight stock use 39

Figures (continued)

Page

Figure 31. Change in number of sites impacted by camping and weighted value per campable mile, between 1976-1981 and 2006-2007, by whether or not campfires are allowed 40

Figure 32. Change in number of sites impacted by camping and weighted value per campable mile, between 1976-1981 and 2006-2007, by whether or not food lockers are provided 40

Figure 33. Scatterplot relating change in campsite impact to initial campsite impact for each subzone 43

Tables

Page

Table 1. Trends in use distribution (overnight visits) among high-use trailheads between the 1970s and the 2000s...5

Table 2. Trends in use distribution: the 15 most heavily used travel zones (visitor nights) in the 1970s and the 2000s...6

Table 3. Criteria and rating factors used to assess campsite condition. 11

Table 4. Descriptive information collected in addition to campsite condition. 12

Table 5. Number of sites impacted by camping, by condition class for sites still being used and referenced as restoration sites for those no longer being used, 2006-2007. 19

Table 6. Number of campsites by condition class, by distance of the campsite from water, 2006-2007. 21

Table 7. Number of campsites by condition class for different overstory types, 2006-2007...22

Table 8. Number of campsites by condition class by degree of canopy cover for forested campsites, 2006-2007...23

Table 9. Number of campsites by condition class and mean site impact for different understory types, 2006-2007...25

Table 10. Number of campsites by condition class by distance of the campsite from a food storage locker, 2006-2007. 25

Table 11. Number of campsites by condition class by firewood availability class, 2006-2007. Firewood availability classes vary from 1 (very abundant, similar to undisturbed conditions) to 5 (very sparse or absent). 26

Table 12. Number of campsites by condition class on sites with various levels of evident stock impact on or around the campsite, 2006-2007...27

Table 13. Change in the number and condition of campsites and all sites impacted by camping, in the subzones sampled in 2006-2007. 31

Table 14. Multiple regression results for variables that influence change in total campsite impact (weighted value). 41

Appendices

Page

Appendix 1: Number and condition of campsites in 2006-2007 59

Appendix 2: Summary campsite impact statistics for each subzone, 2006-2007 65

Appendix 3: Campsite impact by subzone, ordered beginning with those with the
lowest weighted value per campable mile 71

Appendix 4: Number of campsites at various distances from water, 2006-2007 77

Appendix 5: Change in number and condition of campsites since the late 1970s 83

Appendix 6: Change in campsite impact by subzone, ordered beginning with those
with the greatest proportional decrease in aggregate impact 89

Appendix 7: Campsite Monitoring Recommendations and Procedures 95

Appendix 8: Sample Maps of Campsites 101

Executive Summary

In the late 1970s, in response to rapidly increasing visitor use and proliferating impacts, the condition of all campsites in the backcountry of Sequoia and Kings Canyon National Parks was assessed by park research staff. All campsites were located and assigned to one of 273 different subzones; their condition was assessed on the basis of eight impact parameters: vegetation density, vegetation composition, total area of the campsite, barren core area, campsite development, litter and duff, social trails, and tree mutilations. In 2006 and 2007, to ascertain trends in impact, the campsite survey was repeated in 120 of the 273 subzones (44% of the wilderness).

A total of 2,955 sites impacted by camping were located during the 2006-2007 surveys. Of these, 1,795 were judged to be active campsites, with another 1,160 judged to be restoration sites. Restoration sites are sites that appear to no longer be used for camping but where campsite impact is still evident. Since the repeat sample included 44% of the subzones originally surveyed, this suggests that there are approximately 6600 impacted sites in the wilderness, of which about 4000 are being actively used as campsites. In the late 1970s, there were more than 7700 campsites in the wilderness.

In 2006-2007, most of the campsites in the wilderness were not highly impacted. Just considering active campsites, 60% were rated as class 1 campsites. Class 1 campsites range from sites that are barely noticeable to sites that, although small, have clearly been trampled and/or may have fire rings. Another 30% of campsites were rated as class 2 sites. Class 2 sites are obvious campsites that do not appear highly worn. Only 7% of campsites were rated class 3. Class 3 sites are well-impacted popular sites, without attributes of severe impact. Only 2% of campsites were rated as class 4 sites and no campsites were rated class 5. Class 4 sites are highly-impacted, with some aspects of extreme impact. They often have large areas completely devoid of vegetation, litter and duff. When restoration sites are considered as well, about 70 percent of sites can be considered lightly impacted (all class 1 campsites and most restoration sites). Only about 6% of sites (perhaps 350 sites in the entire wilderness) are substantially impacted (class 3 and 4 campsites) and no sites have the extreme levels of impact found on class 5 sites in the initial survey.

In the late 1970s as well, most campsites were not highly impacted. However, there were more sites with substantial impact that in 2006-2007. The distribution of condition classes in the late 1970s was 37% class 1 sites, 34% class 2 sites, 18% class 3 sites, 7% class 4 sites and 4% class 5 sites. In the late 1970s, there were 329 class 5 sites in the entire wilderness.

The most important finding of this study is that **campsite conditions in the wilderness of Sequoia and Kings Canyon National Parks have improved dramatically since the late 1970s**. Depending on assumptions and the comparability of the two surveys, aggregate campsite impact in 2006-2007 is almost certainly less than one-third what it was in the 1970s. No other wildernesses where trends in impact have been studied have improved so dramatically. But conversely, no other wildernesses had the high level of impact that existed here in the 1970s.

The second fundamental finding is that **the improvement in conditions that has occurred over the past 30 years has been remarkably uniform**. With only a few localized exceptions, conditions have improved throughout the wilderness of Sequoia and Kings Canyon National Parks. Despite concerns to the contrary, impacts are not spreading or intensifying; they have retreated and diminished in magnitude. Near-pristine wilderness is not disappearing; it may be expanding. The installation of bear-proof food storage lockers in the 1980s may have intensified use in the immediate vicinity of lockers. However, the sites selected for lockers were usually places that were already highly impacted. Given increased use of Leave-No-Trace and minimum impact techniques, these sites are often in better condition now than they were in the past, even if use intensity has increased. Food storage lockers have had no apparent effect on campsite impact at the scale of the subzone.

Campsite impacts are not equitably distributed. They are more substantial along primary trails, particularly the John Muir Trail, and they are concentrated both in popular subzones (e.g. the Rae Lakes) and within subzones, at trail junctions, creek crossings and along lakeshores. However, because the most highly impacted places are the ones that have improved the most, the disparity between more and less impacted places has actually decreased. In the 1970s, campsite impact decreased significantly with increases in elevation, distance from the trailhead and distance from the closest ranger station. Campsite impact no longer varies with any of these factors.

There are several competing potential explanations for the decrease in campsite impact over the past 30 years. There is evidence that use levels are not as high today as they were in the 1970s. There is also evidence that use is more concentrated in space than it was in the 1970s. Although the relationship between impact and the spatial distribution of use is complex, total impact is often less where use is concentrated rather than more widely distributed (Hammitt and Cole 1998). Visitor behavior has also changed. There has been widespread adoption of minimum impact techniques, including Leave-No-Trace, and some of the activities with high impact potential (e.g. campfire building and traveling with large packstock groups) are more tightly regulated. Finally, in the period between the two surveys, there was a concerted on-the-ground management effort to reduce campsite impacts. It is our contention that all of these factors have contributed to improvement in conditions and have worked synergistically toward improved conditions. However, we also believe that **the most important of these reasons for success has been the concerted effort and hard work of wilderness managers and rangers to reduce campsite impact throughout the wilderness**. The fundamental strategy that evolved was to concentrate use on a smaller number of campsites, in appropriate locations, work to reduce campsite size and development, more actively maintain campsites, and educate visitors. Specific actions taken to implement this strategy included:

- obliterating unnecessary campsites when there are plenty of others around,
- eliminating sites too close to water, particularly those within 25 feet,
- eliminating campsite developments, such as built up tables, rock walls, etc.
- building small fire rings at certain campsites and maintaining them,
- reducing the size of very large sites,
- constantly eliminating campfire evidence where fires are illegal, and
- educating visitors about how to minimize their impact.

This multi-faceted approach, directed by wilderness managers and implemented by wilderness rangers, has succeeded in substantially improving the wilderness character of the Sequoia and Kings Canyon Wilderness.

Acknowledgments

Many people contributed to the work described in this report and to all of them we are thankful. Gregg Fauth conceived the project, advocated for it and secured funding for it. He hired and supervised the crews that worked in the field and did data entry and he helped us gather useful supplementary information and reports. This project would not have been possible without Gregg's foresight and efforts. Financial and in-kind support was provided by both the National Park Service and the Aldo Leopold Wilderness Research Institute, USDA Forest Service, Rocky Mountain Research Station. We also particularly appreciate the work of Sandy Graban who coordinated and did much of the reinventory fieldwork and initial data entry. She was ably assisted in the field by Amanda Marusich, Bob Kenan and others, including the wilderness rangers, and in the office by Rose Cook, Yoshi Terai, Peter Stephens, Pat Lineback, Sylvia Haultain and undoubtedly others. Thanks to Chris Stalling of the Forest Service, in Missoula, for producing the sample maps included in Appendix 8 and the additional maps of all the sites included in our original report that were too numerous to provide in this publication. We thank Gregg Fauth, Sandy Graban, Alison Steiner, Nate Stephenson and Sylvia Haultain for their thoughtful reviews of our manuscript. This project would not have been possible without the foresight and work of those who conducted the initial inventory, many of whom are named in Parsons and Stohlgren (1987). Finally, we dedicate this report to the wilderness managers and rangers who have labored over the past 30 years to ensure that the story we have to tell is such a positive one.

Introduction

Sequoia and Kings Canyon National Parks are among the premier destinations in the world for wilderness travel and camping. Over 93% of the spectacular mountain country that make up these parks has been designated as wilderness, with another 4% managed as wilderness. The parks are home to the highest peak in the lower 48 states, Mt. Whitney (14,495 feet), a 97-mile stretch of the famous John Muir Trail and also 101 miles of the Pacific Crest Trail. In all, there are more than 700 miles of maintained trail in the parks, as well as numerous opportunities to travel off trails. Wilderness recreation has a long history here; a number of scenic attractions have been popular destinations for over a century. Due to this popularity, Sequoia and Kings Canyon National Parks pioneered efforts to sustainably manage wilderness recreation and this management program remains in the vanguard today.

Much of the wilderness management effort has been devoted to minimizing the substantial adverse environmental effects of wilderness recreation use, particularly those associated with camping. As has been well-documented, camping causes a variety of ecological impacts, in addition to having social and aesthetic impacts. Aesthetic and social impacts include the effects on solitude and privacy of encountering other campers, as well as seeing evidence of prior use that detracts from the natural scene. In some places, wilderness travelers encounter conditions perceived to reflect inappropriate behavior, such as campsites marred by litter, waste from humans and stock, or excessive "development", particularly large fire rings and rock walls. Common ecological impacts include (1) damage to standing trees from firewood collection, tying stock to trees and thoughtless or vandalous acts, (2) destruction of understory vegetation, loss of litter and duff and compaction of mineral soils due to trampling, and (3) elimination of downed woody debris used as firewood (Stohlgren and Parsons 1986, Hammitt and Cole 1998).

Given the long history of wilderness recreation at the parks and the substantial impacts associated with camping, campsite management has been a concern for over half a century. As early as 1961, camping was prohibited at Bullfrog Lake on account of excessive impact (Parsons 1979). By 1970, restrictions were imposed at the popular Rae Lakes area; stays at the lakes were limited to one night and campfires were no longer allowed (Parsons 1983). In support of the wilderness management program at the parks, an inventory of all campsites in the wilderness was conducted between 1976 and 1980. During that inventory, conditions were recorded on a total of 7,732 wilderness campsites—2,973 in Sequoia and 4,759 in Kings Canyon (Parsons and Stohlgren 1987). The information collected provided a basis for determination of user capacities in the 1980s, including the trailhead quotas presented in the parks' 1986 Backcountry Management Plan (Parsons 1986).

By the mid-2000s, it had been three decades since the initial inventory of campsites and two decades since implementation of the parks' Backcountry Management and Stock Use and Meadow Management Plans. As part of an effort to revisit and update these plans within a unified Wilderness Stewardship Plan, the decision was made to reinventory campsites in a sample of the parks 'wilderness to describe current conditions and assess trends. This monograph reports the results of that reassessment of campsite distribution and condition. Specific objectives of the report are (1) to describe the current condition of wilderness campsites, (2) describe how conditions have changed over the past 30 years, (3) explore potential reasons for the change that occurred and (4) discuss the management implications of our findings.

Study Area

Sequoia and Kings Canyon National Parks are located in the southern Sierra Nevada of California. The wilderness of the two parks consist of the 768,222 acre Sequoia-Kings Canyon Wilderness and the largely-contiguous 39,740 acre John Krebs Wilderness. These lands are bounded by Forest Service wilderness on the north, east and south and portions of the west—making them part of one of the largest blocks of wilderness in the lower 48 states. These wildernesses are accessed by over 70 trailheads, both on park land and adjacent Forest Service land.

Sites impacted by camping are located in a wide range of vegetation types, at elevations from below 5000 feet in the canyon bottoms of the west to over 14,000 feet on the summit of Mt. Whitney. Most sites are located in the mixed coniferous forest of mid-elevations, the extensive coniferous forest of the subalpine zone or within the mosaic of forest and meadow that occurs close to timberline; however, there are also many campsites in the open alpine communities above timberline, as well as some below the coniferous forest.

Visitor Use

Obtaining accurate counts of visitor use is a challenge, due to the dispersion of access points, the need to share information across agency boundaries and the number of people who do not obtain permits or who change their route or length of stay once on a trip. This makes it difficult to precisely describe use trends, despite the exemplary effort the parks have made to collect use data. There is little dispute about the fact that current use is much higher than it was prior to the 1970s and that it is lower than it was during the backpacking boom years of the 1970s (Figure 1). However, as will be discussed in more detail later, there are reasons to mistrust the magnitude of change in use suggested by Figure 1. Year-to-year, use levels fluctuate dramatically but have generally been increasing recently. The long-term trend can be characterized as one of ever-increasing use, with a notable spike in use that began by the late 1960s and ended in the 1980s. Permit data show a peak in overnight use of about 220,000 visitor nights in 1974, more than four times what it was a decade before and almost twice what it was in 2010. It is important to note that the initial campsite inventory occurred late in the decade during which wilderness use increased most rapidly—at the peak of the backpacking boom. The repeat inventory came after a period of stable or slightly increasing use, at levels well below peak use of the 1970s. Unfortunately, there are no data for conditions prior to the backpacking boom.

Most wilderness use in these parks occurs during the summer—between Memorial Day and mid-September. Most use is backpacking; less than four percent of visitors travel with horses or mules. Mean party size is about three persons and the mean length of stay is three to four days. These use characteristics are little changed from what they were in the 1970s, although typical length of stay has declined somewhat. However, amount of stock use is substantially lower than it was in the 1970s. Total stock use nights during the decade of the 2000s were only about one-half of stock nights in the 1970s. Private stock use, in particular, has declined. The number of private stock use nights during the 2000s was only 38% of private stock nights in the 1970s.

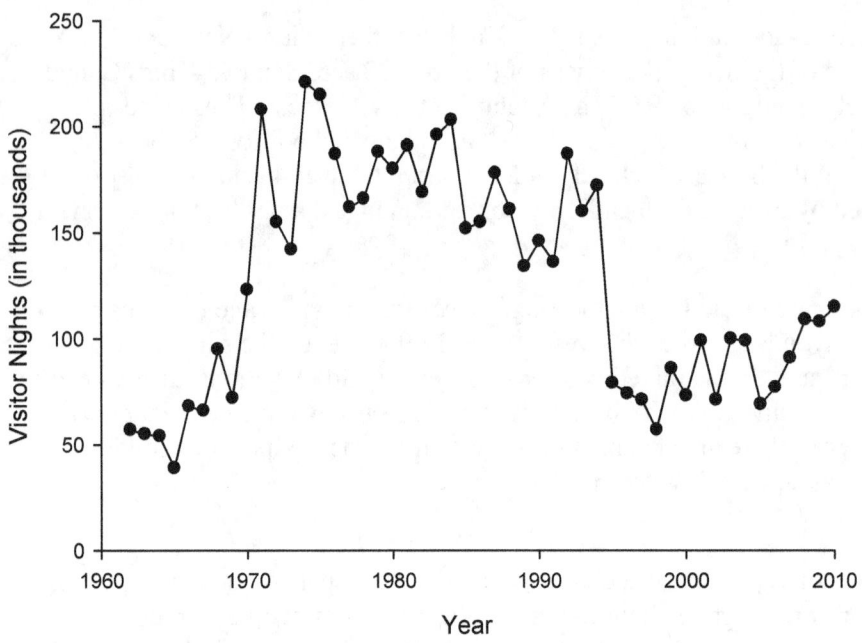

Figure 1. Trends in wilderness use, as reported on wilderness permits.

Use of the wilderness has always been concentrated at a variety of spatial scales. The John Muir Trail, High Sierra Trail and Rae Lakes Loop have been more heavily used than other trails for close to a century. Then, on any given route, there are locations that are particularly popular for camping—trail junctions, meadows with good feed, lakes with good fishing and locations with outstanding scenery. In addition, most travel occurs on maintained trails, although there are abandoned trails and cross-country routes that receive regular use. Finally, there are often particular campsites that are used much more than other campsites in the vicinity. Various forces have influenced the degree to which and where use is concentrated. Guidebooks extolling cross-country routes, information about crowding on the John Muir Trail, quota systems and length-of-stay limits have served to disperse use more widely. Campfire restrictions, bear-proof food storage lockers, designated campsites, packstock restrictions and a reduction in miles of maintained trail maintenance have served to concentrate use. So have guidebooks and information posted on the internet that gives the coordinates of campsites. Visitor education has also had an influence. During the 1970s, much of the message involved spreading out to avoid crowding and impact; more recently, concentrating use on sites that have already been well-impacted has been given more emphasis.

The distribution of use among trailheads has not changed dramatically since the 1970s. Nine of the 10 most popular trailheads in the 1970s are still among the most popular 10 trailheads today (Table 1). The 10 most popular trailheads accounted for 62% of overnight visits in the 1970s and 65% of overnight visits in 2007-2010. The largest changes among popular trailheads are Cottonwood Pass and Trailcrest/Main Whitney. Trailcrest/Main Whitney was the eighth most popular trailhead in the 1970s; today it is the 26th most popular. Apparently, the popularity of the

Mt. Whitney climb and the difficulty of obtaining a permit means that most successful permittees these days do not stay overnight in the parks. The Cottonwood Pass trailhead, in contrast, is currently much more popular (9th) than it was in the 1970s (19th). There are several likely reasons for this. The road into the Cottonwood Pass trailhead was newly-constructed in the 1970s and it may have taken people some time to become aware of it. Reduced quotas for climbing Mt. Whitney caused many to seek an alternate route to access Whitney, with Cottonwood Lakes and Pass providing the most convenient alternative. Moreover, a new section of the Pacific Crest Trail was built in the interim, providing quicker access to lower Rock Creek and the Mt. Whitney region. To some degree, decreased use of the park west of Mt. Whitney, by visitors using Trailcrest/Main Whitney, has been offset by increased use of the Cottonwood Pass trailhead and by through hikers on the John Muir Trail.

Table 1. Trends in use distribution (overnight visits) among high-use trailheads between the 1970s and the 2000s.

Trailhead	Percent of Total Use (2007-10)	Rank	Percent of Total Use (1971-78)	Rank
Kearsarge Pass	10.4	1	9.1	1
Woods Creek	8.8	2	8.0	2
High Sierra Trail/Bearpaw	8.1	3	6.4	6
Bishop Pass	8.0	4	6.7	5
Bubbs Creek	6.0	5	6.8	4
Pear Lake	5.8	6	5.6	7
Cottonwood Lakes	4.9	7	3.7	10
Twin Lakes	4.8	8	6.9	3
Cottonwood Pass	4.3	9	3.7	19
Alta	3.8	10	4.1	9

One trend not apparent in these data is the dramatic increase in number of people hiking the entire John Muir Trail. John Muir Trail hikers are not counted with the accuracy of other hikers and were not included in the data presented in Tables 1 or 2. Since 1998, when about 300 people hiked the entire trail, there has been a six-fold increase in hikers. In 2010, people hiking the entire John Muir Trail accounted for about 7% of overnight visits in the park wilderness (number of people who stayed overnight). Since most of these people hike from north to south, this trend has resulted in a substantial increase in the number of people entering the parks along the South Fork of the San Joaquin River. Whereas perhaps 7% of visitors entered there in the 1970s, the proportion entering there now may be as high as 12%. If so, this entry point has replaced Kearsarge Pass as the most heavily-used entry point to the park wilderness. Conversely, some relatively quiet portions of the wilderness have become even less frequently used. The Hockett Plateau is a good example. Trailheads accessing the southwestern corner of the wilderness accounted for more than 3% of total use in the 1970s; today, barely 1% of visitation occurs in this area.

The use distribution among travel zones appears to have changed more dramatically, although these data are much more subject to inaccuracies resulting from reporting procedures. Only 8 of the 15 most heavily-used travel zones in the late 1970s were still among the most popular travel zones in 2007-2010 (Table 2). Travel zone use distribution, like trailhead use distribution, has become slightly more concentrated. The 15 most popular travel zones accounted for 56% of total use in the late 1970s and 61% of total use in 2007-2010. The 10 travel zones with the largest increases in relative use are Crabtree, Rock Creek, Evolution Basin, Rae Lakes, Tyndall Creek, Upper Basin, Kearsarge Lakes, LeConte Canyon and Palisade Basin.

Table 2. Trends in use distribution: the 15 most heavily used travel zones (visitor nights) in the 1970s and the 2000s.

Travel Zone	Percent of Total Use (2007-10)	Travel Zone	Percent of Total Use (1976-79)
Middle Fork Kaweah	8.4	Middle Fork Kaweah	9.2
Crabtree	6.9	Rattlesnake Creek	5.7
Dusy Basin	4.9	Paradise Valley	4.6
Rae Lakes	4.8	Hockett Meadow	4.0
Rock Creek	4.5	McClure Meadow	3.5
Evolution Basin	4.2	Pear Lake	3.4
Pear Lake	4.0	Bubbs Creek	3.3
Paradise Valley	3.7	Seville Lake	3.2
Bubbs Creek	3.5	Goddard Canyon	3.0
Center Basin-Vidette	2.8	Big Five Lakes	2.9
LeConte Canyon	2.8	Mt. Silliman	2.7
Kearsarge Lakes	2.7	Moose Lake	2.8
Mt. Silliman	2.7	Granite Basin	2.7
Tyndall Creek	2.6	Rae Lakes	2.6
Rattlesnake Creek	2.6	Dusy Basin	2.5

Clearly, there has been a shift in use toward the John Muir Trail and travel zones close to Mt. Whitney. Nine of the 14 travel zones that the John Muir Trail passes through are among the 12 zones that increased most. The 10 travel zones with the largest decreases in relative use are Rattlesnake Creek, Hockett Meadow, Goddard Canyon, Granite Basin, Moose Lake, McClure Meadow, State Lakes, Big Five Lakes, Paradise Valley and Kennedy Pass. This is a more disparate set of travel zones, but concentrated around the Monarch Divide, the Roaring River country and the southwestern corner of Sequoia National Park. Much of this country was traditional packstock country that may be seeing less use as packstock use declines.

Visitor Use Management

As noted above, some of the trends in use distribution reflect changes in management. Prior to the 1970s, visitor use management was largely confined to routine patrol and campsite clean-up. Considerable energy was consumed dealing with trash, particularly large can dumps remaining from the era when burying trash was advised. But the need for more active management in popular places was becoming clear. Bullfrog Lake was closed to camping in 1961 (Parsons 1979) and camping restrictions at Rae Lakes were implemented in 1970. By 1976, the time the initial campsite inventory was initiated, overnight use limits had been established throughout the wilderness. Quotas were established for every trailhead, limiting the number of people per day that could enter the wilderness (Parsons et al. 1981). Once they gained access, they could travel wherever they wanted. These limits were first put into effect in 1972 for the Rae Lakes Loop and expanded to both parks in 1975 (Parsons 1983).

By the mid-1970s, special camping restrictions, including prohibitions on campfires, had been established in a number of specific problem areas. Camping was not allowed at four lakes-- Bullfrog, Heather, Aster and Timberline--and was only allowed at designated sites at Pear and Emerald Lakes. There was also a one-night limit on camping along the Rae Lakes Loop at Rae Lakes, Sixty Lakes Basin, Charlotte Lake, Kearsarge Lakes, Dragon Lake, Dollar Lake and along the John Muir Trail between Woods Creek and Glen Pass. Campfires were prohibited in seven specific locations: Evolution Basin, from Evolution Lake to Muir Pass; Dusy Basin, from Bishop Pass to Upper Bridge on the Dusy Branch Trail; Kearsarge Lakes; Pear, Emerald, Heather and Aster Lakes; Twin Lakes; Rae Lakes, from Dollar Lake to Glen Pass; and Sphinx Lakes above 10,000 feet.

A number of stock use restrictions were also implemented (McClaran 1989). By the mid-1970s, all stock travel was prohibited in four places (Crabtree Lakes, lower Kearsarge-Bullfrog trail, McGee Lakes, and from one mile above Guitar Lake to Mt. Whitney summit); three places were closed to overnight use (Pear Lake, Moose Lake, and Timberline Lake) and ten places were closed to grazing (Junction Meadow on Bubbs Creek, Guitar Lake, Bubbs Creek, East Lake, Paradise Valley, Rae Lakes, upper Charlotte and meadow below lake, Kearsarge-Bullfrog, Dusy Basin, and Evolution Lake). Five meadows were closed to grazing before a particular date (Upper and Lower Funston, Vidette Meadow, McClure Meadow, and Colby Meadow) and eleven meadows had length of stay limits (Redwood Meadow, South Fork Meadow, Tuohy Meadow, Upper and Lower Funston, Scaffold Meadow, Cement Table, Castle Domes Meadow, Sixty Lakes Basin, Charlotte Creek, and Vidette Meadow).

By the mid-1980s, the number of places with campsite, campfire and stock restrictions had increased. Camping was prohibited in three new places: (1) at Eagle Lake, between trail and lake, (2) at Mosquito Lake #1, within 100 feet of the lake and (3) between the trail and Whitman Creek at the Hockett Meadow Camps. Camping was confined to designated sites in Paradise Valley and length-of-stay limits were imposed there and at Hamilton Lakes. Site-specific campfire restrictions were generally replaced by elevational restrictions: above 10,000 feet in Kings Canyon and also in Granite Basin; above 11,200 feet in the Kern Canyon; and above 9,000 feet in the Kaweah drainage and also at Hamilton Lakes. New restrictions on stock use included a program of opening dates for grazing that varied depending on moisture conditions. Overall stock use was to be limited to the 1977-1984 average. Nineteen meadows continued to be closed to grazing due to prior impact, while another 13 areas had limits on length of stay (either one or

7

two nights) and 8 areas limited number of stock to 15. Unrestricted off-trail stock use was disallowed in some management zones, which resulted in the closure of another 23 named forage areas to grazing; this restriction meant an additional 34% of all meadow areas were off-limits to pack stock. Finally, a network of 14 meadows was closed to all grazing to serve as undisturbed controls.

In addition, by the late 1970s the wilderness rangers gave increased emphasis to efforts to improve campsite conditions. Over time, this effort evolved into a program of reducing, relocating and actively maintaining campsites. The latter program was facilitated by information gleaned from the initial campsite survey. In particular, campsites were eliminated if they were too close to water; ideally sites were to be at least 50 feet from water. Sites were also eliminated if there were more than necessary in any location. Fire rings were eliminated in places where campfires were no longer allowed. In addition, developments such as tables and seats were eliminated and large fire rings were replaced with smaller fire rings. Attempts were made to reduce the size of extremely large campsites.

Another significant management change that occurred during the 1980s involved the installation of food storage devices to help visitors keep food away from bears. Initially, bear cables and poles were used. But these were quickly replaced by food storage lockers. Currently, there are 82 food storage lockers located at popular destinations along trails in the southern portion of Kings Canyon National Park and throughout Sequoia National Park. These lockers serve to concentrate use on campsites close to the lockers.

Substantial progress was made during the late 1970s and 1980s in reducing the number, size and level of development of sites, as well as campfire evidence where fires are prohibited. This focus was a shift in emphasis from the 1960s and early 1970s, when trash removal was a much more significant task. Maintaining the fruits of these efforts requires constant vigilance. Despite increased knowledge about leave-no-trace techniques and general compliance with regulations, some visitors still build new campsites and have fires in places where they are prohibited. These sites need to be dismantled. Moreover at popular sites, where campfires are still allowed, ashes need to be removed. Wilderness rangers report that, ideally, popular sites need to be cleaned once every two weeks. This work is the responsibility of wilderness rangers who are diligent in providing these services, along with educating visitors in minimum impact practices.

Methods

The results reported here come from (1) an initial survey of all parts of the wilderness of both parks between 1976 and 1981 and (2) a repeat survey of almost one-half of these areas in 2006 and 2007. To facilitate reporting of campsite distribution and impact data, the parks' 52 travel zones were subdivided into 273 different subzones—originally referred to as management areas. Most travel zones have four to six subzones, though some have as few as two and one has 15. Subzones are smaller, more ecologically homogeneous areas that can be managed more consistently than the larger travel zones.

The Initial Survey, 1976-1981

Field crew members attempted to locate all campsites along established trails, many of the more popular cross-country routes and at likely camping destinations, such as trail-less lakes. They documented campsite attributes and conditions using the methodology described by Parsons and MacLeod (1980). Although the survey extended from 1976 to 1981, it was virtually complete after the 1979 season. Surveyors wandered around searching some distance from trails and water bodies in an effort to find as many campsites as possible. Campsites were defined as any sites showing evidence of past overnight use. These include sites with fire rings or with cleared areas suitable for sleeping. While some were small and lightly impacted, others were large and highly developed. In some popular areas, clusters of individual sites coalesce, making it difficult to determine whether there is one large site or a number of smaller sites. The number of individual sites in a cluster was based on a judgment of how many independent groups might camp there on a single night.

In the initial survey, each campsite was located on a sketch map of the immediate area. Back in the office, each campsite was represented by a dot on 1:62,500 scale USGS quadrangle maps. In addition, the condition of each campsite was assessed and other locational and descriptive information was noted. Campsite condition was assessed on the basis of eight criteria. The parameters used were:

- Density of Vegetation: A relative measure of the extent of vegetative ground cover within the campsite compared with similar unimpacted areas outside the site.

- Composition of Vegetation: A measure comparing the species composition and relative abundance in the campsite to surrounding unimpacted areas.

- Total Area of the Campsite: An estimate of the total area affected by trampling directly associated with use in and about the site.

- Barren Core: An estimate of the area that had been completely denuded of vegetation by trampling. This usually was confined to the central part of the campsite.

- Campsite Development: A rating based on the amount of man-made "improvement" in the campsite, such as tables, rock walls, fire rings, etc.

- Litter and Duff: Applied only on forested sites, this is a rating of the degree to which organic debris (needles, cones and twigs) had been pulverized or removed by trampling and other use.

- Social Trails: a measure of impact on surrounding vegetation from trampling of informal access trails to such nearby destinations as water sources, main trails, other campsites, etc.

- Mutilations: Applied only in wooded areas, a measure of the number of permanent marks on trees, such as carving, axe marks and nails.

Rating factors for each criterion are presented in Table 3. Factors were based on a five point scale, with five representing maximum impact. Level one represented minimal impact. The values recorded for each of the applicable criteria (as applied to that site) were summed and divided by the number of criteria to produce an overall condition class rating. With practice, surveyors were able to assign a condition class rating without recording ratings for individual criteria. In the interest of saving time, this approach was taken on the majority of sites. Individual criteria were recorded for about 20% of the sites.

In addition, the following descriptive information was recorded: overstory and understory vegetation type and cover, distance to water, and the number of other class 3, 4, and 5 sites within 100 feet (an indicator of crowding potential). An evaluation was made of the site's potential for use by large groups and comments were recorded on such items as the number of fire rings and fire scars and the need for rehabilitation or other management action. Table 4 shows descriptive information collected when the survey was repeated. It included some information not collected in the initial survey.

In addition to campsite-specific data, descriptive information was recorded for each subzone. This included elevation, landform (lake, river valley, ridge, plateau, etc.), potential campable area (an estimate of the proportion of the area amenable to camping), the percent of campable area currently used for camping, overstory vegetation type and cover, whether meadows constitute a significant portion of the area, and a qualitative rating of firewood availability. In the office, maps and use data were consulted to identify the trail type that was used by most people to access the subzone (primary or secondary trail, unmaintained footpath or cross-country). The distance to the nearest trailhead, the trailhead contributing the majority of use and the nearest ranger station were also recorded.

Table 3. Criteria and rating factors used to assess campsite condition.

Vegetation Criteria and Rating Factors	
Vegetation Density (with respect to surrounding vegetation) 1 = same as surroundings 3 = moderately less dense than surroundings 5 = considerably less dense than surroundings	**Vegetation Composition** (with respect to surrounding vegetation) 1 = same as surroundings 3 = moderately dissimilar 5 = significantly dissimilar
Physical Area Criteria and Rating Factors	
Total Area of Campsite 1 = less than or equal to 20 square feet (2 sq. meters) 2 = 21 – 100 square feet (2 – 9 sq. meters) 3 = 101 – 500 square feet (9 – 47 sq. meters) 4 = 501 – 1,000 square feet (93 square meters) 5 = greater than 1,001 square feet	**Barren Core Area** 1 = absent 2 = 5 – 50 square feet 3 = 51 – 200 square feet 4 = 201 – 500 square feet 5 = greater than 501 square feet
Campsite Development	
1 = windbreaks & paraphernalia absent, trash & seats minimal; firerings absent or scarce 2 = trash, windbreaks, seats, and firerings minimal; paraphernalia absent 3 = trash, windbreaks, seats mostly moderate; firerings mostly minimal; paraphernalia minimal 4 = trash, windbreaks, seats, and paraphernalia mostly moderate; firerings mostly minimal; some heavy 5 = trash, windbreaks, seats, firerings, paraphernalia mostly heavily developed	
Litter and Duff	
1 = trampling barely discernible; some needles broken; scattered cones 2 = moderately trampled; needles broken; compacted; few cones 3 = heavily trampled; clumped; pulverized; cones absent 4 = litter more or less absent; pulverized; ground into soil 5 = litter, cones, and duff completely absent	
Other Criteria and Rating Factors	
Social Trails 1 = None 2 = 1 trail discernible 3 = 2 trails discernible 4 = 1-2 trails well-developed or >3 trails more or less discernible 5 = >3 well-developed trails	**Mutilations (mostly tree damage)** 1 = none 2 = 1-2 3 = 3-5 4 = 6-10 or 1-2 highly obtrusive 5= >11 or 3 more or less highly obtrusive

Table 4. Descriptive information collected in addition to campsite condition.

Site History	Site Potential (Management Recommendations)
1 = normal, on-going use 2 = ongoing use, but evidence of rehabilitation (rehabilitated from more severe condition in the past) 3 = new site; mainly 1's or 2's (Qualify in comments section)	1 = **MT** = maintain as is 2 = **MT/S** = maintain as is/potential stock site 3 = **C** = Containment (rehabilitation, etc.) 4 = **OBL** = Obliterate
Overstory Type	**Overstory Cover**
01 = **LP** = Lodgepole Pine 02 = **WB** = Whitebark Pine 03 = **FT** = Foxtail Pine 04 = **LP+WB** = Lodgepole-Whitebark 05 = **LP+FT** = Lodgepole-Foxtail 06 = **WB+LP** = Whitebark-Lodgepole 07 = **FT+LP** = Foxtail-Lodgepole 08 = MM = Montane-Mixed Conifer (includes Red Fir, Jeffrey Pine, White Fir, Sugar Pine, Incense Cedar and Black Oak) 09 = **SubM** = Subalpine-Mixed Conifer (includes Lodgepole Foxtail, Whitebark and Western White Pine; and Mountain Hemlock) 10 = **XM** = Xeric-Mixed Conifer (includes Lodgepole Pine, Western Juniper, Red Fir, Jeffrey Pine, and Foxtail Pine) 11 = **Alp** = Alpine (Open) 12 = **RF** = Red Fir 13 = **Other**	1 = **O** = Open 2 = **Int** = Intermediate 3 = **C** = Closed 4 = **M** = Mosaic 5 = **B** = Barren 6 = **Other** (describe)
Understory Type	**Understory Cover**
01 = Carex 02 = Grass and Sedge 03 = Grass and Herb 04 = Herb and Grass 05 = Barren Soil 06 = Rock and Gravel 07 = Duff 08 = Shrub	1 = <5% 2 = 5-25% 3 = 26-50% 4 = 51-75% 5 = 76-95% 6 = 96-100%
Stock Impacts	**Crowding**
0 = None 1 = Light; sparse pawing and manure 2 = Moderate pawing/manure/exposed roots 3 = Severe pawing/manure/exposed roots	# of condition class 3, 4, 5 sites within 100 feet of other condition class 3, 4, 5 sites
Distance to Food Storage Box	**Distance to Water**
1 = greater than 500 feet (152.4 meters) 2 = 250-500 feet (76.2 – 152.4 meters) 3 = 100-250 feet (30.48-76.2 meters) 4 = 50-100 feet (15.24-30.48 meters) NA = 5 = >1 mile or subjectively too far for use by campers	1 = >100 feet (30.5 meters) 2 = 50-100 feet (15-30.5 meters) 3 = 25-50 feet (7.6-15 meters) 4 = 0-25 feet (0-7.6 meters)

Table 4. Descriptive information collected in addition to campsite condition (continued).

Firewood Availability
1 = ground fuel **very abundant or similar to nearby (control) areas**; dean and downed wood very abundant within or immediately adjacent (within 25 yards) of camp area.
2 = ground fuel **abundant**; dead and downed wood abundant within 100 yards of camp areas or moderately reduced from nearby areas.
3 = ground fuel **intermediate**; dead and downed wood sparse to scattered within or immediately adjacent to camp area. Scattered to moderately available within 150 yards. Moderately available to abundant beyond.
4 = ground fuel **sparse**; dead and downed fuels absent or very sparse within and immediately adjacent to camp area. Occasional pockets of sparse to moderate fuels may occur. Very sparse to scattered within 200 yards of camp area. Scattered to moderately available beyond.
5 = ground fuel **very sparse to absent**; dead and downed fuels absent from immediate vicinity of camp area. Very sparse for a distance of >200 yards. Firewood obviously carried in from long distance (>1/8 mile).

The Repeat Survey, 2006-2007

In 2006 and 2007, the campsite survey was repeated in 120 (44%) of the 273 subzones. In 2006, all 54 subzones in 9 purposely-selected travel zones were surveyed (Figure 2). The travel zones selected (McClure Meadow, LeConte Canyon, Rae Lakes, Charlotte Lake, Kearsarge Lakes, Funston Meadow, Crabtree, Rock Creek and Army Pass) were primarily popular zones where changes were expected based on management actions taken and/or changes in visitor behavior and use patterns. Another 9 subzones, located in 5 different travel zones were surveyed in 2006; many of these were less popular locations. In 2007, this sample was supplemented with a random sample of 57 other subzones. So the repeat sample can be characterized as a very large sample that is slightly biased toward more popular use areas.

Perhaps the most fundamental change in procedure in the repeat survey regarded the treatment of sites that had not been recently camped on. Instead of considering them to be campsites, they were recorded as restoration sites—sites that still showed the impacts of camping but had either been actively restored or appeared to be abandoned and not used for many years. For each restoration site, GPS coordinates were recorded and it was noted whether the site had been closed and actively restored by rangers or whether it was recovering on its own because nobody chooses to camp there. As will be discussed further, in the data analysis section, this change in procedure limits the comparability of the two data sets—a limitation that can be minimized by making certain assumptions about the data.

Comparability is also reduced slightly by the fact that surveyors did not necessarily cover exactly the same ground in each period. During the repeat survey, field workers had the benefit of the site maps from the earlier survey. There are a handful of places (portions of 7 different subzones) where it is clear that the 2006-2007 survey reached places that were missed in the initial survey. Overall, we believe that the repeat survey was a slightly more complete survey.

Comparability is also reduced by the fact that evaluations were conducted by different field workers in the two time periods. This issue was recognized early on and substantial effort went

13

into maximizing comparability. For example, evaluations were calibrated in the field with one member of the initial field crew. Although it is difficult to prove, we believe that condition class ratings in the repeat survey were probably slightly lower than in the initial survey. We discuss this in more detail later.

For the 2006-2007 survey, the same criteria were used to assign condition class ratings to each campsite (Table 3). Individual criteria were assessed for all sites that appeared to have ratings of class 3 or higher, as well as some more lightly impacted sites. In all, individual criteria were recorded for 35% of sites, compared to 20% in the initial survey. For most sites, it was impossible to determine if the site was a new site or a particular site from the initial survey. However, GPS coordinates were recorded for each site, so such a determination should be possible in subsequent surveys. The amount of campsite-specific information was increased in the repeat survey. Information added included: management history, distance to a food storage locker, number of firepits, firewood availability, and evidence of stock impacts.

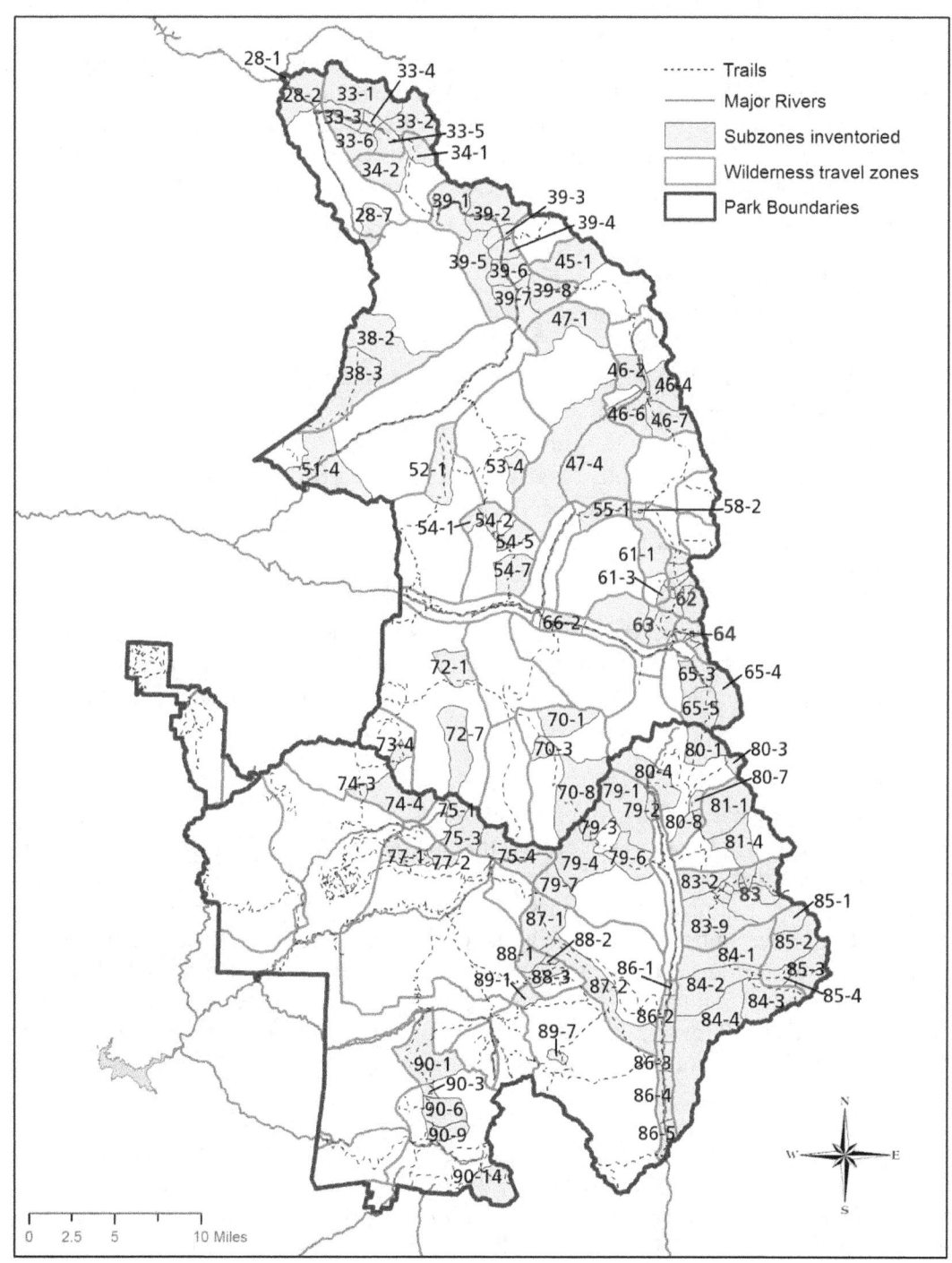

Figure 2. Map of Sequoia and Kings Canyon National Parks showing the subzones that were inventoried in 2006-2007. Subzones in travel zones 62, 63, 64 and 83 were too small to label separately.

15

Field Trips and Interviews

In addition, the two authors of this report took two trips into the wilderness to make observations of how conditions relate to data collected. Among other things, these trips allowed the authors to assess the thoroughness of the reinventory and its compatibility with the initial survey. On each trip, we were accompanied by the lead person on the reinventory (Sandy Graban) and/or wilderness rangers who assisted in the reinventory (Alison Steiner and Rob Pilewski). We also interviewed long-term wilderness rangers and others with a long history of working and observing conditions in the wilderness of the parks, some dating from the 1970s. Those interviewed included:

- George Durkee, Wilderness Ranger
- Dave Gordon, Wilderness Ranger
- David Graber, Chief Scientist, Pacific West Region
- David Karplus, Trails Supervisor, Kings Canyon National Park
- Dario Malengo, Wilderness Ranger
- Rob Pilewski, Wilderness Ranger
- Nate Stephenson, Research Ecologist, USGS Sequoia-Kings Canyon Field Station
- Bill Tweed, Chief of Interpretation (retired)
- Harold Werner, Wildlife Ecologist (retired)
- Cindy Wood, Wilderness Ranger

We asked questions about observed changes in conditions, potential reasons for the changes observed, types of management actions that were taken and how management relates to change in conditions. These interviews informed the discussion and conclusions presented in this report.

Data Analysis

To compare campsite conditions in different subzones, a procedure for arriving at an aggregate impact rating for each subzone was needed. Although the mean condition class rating was one option, it was clear that the rating scale of one to five was not linear. A class five site is much more than five times as impacted as a class one site. To arrive at a more appropriate rating scale, it was decided to use campsite area as the basis for the weighting scale. Specifically, weights were the ratios between the campsite area midpoints from the five classes in Table 3. The results were "weighted value" ratings of 1 for a class 1 site, 6 for a class 2 site, 30 for a class 3 site, 75 for a class 4 site and 150 for a class 5 site. Using these ratings, the aggregate impact for each subzone (total weighted value) was calculated by summing the weighted values of all the campsites in the subzone.

The second issue that had to be dealt with was the vastly different size of the subzones. A subzone with a large total weighted value might be either an area with unusually high levels of campsite impact or a very large subzone. For example, it was common to divide highly-impacted places into smaller subzones. The comparability of subzones was increased by estimating the "campable miles" of each subzone. This metric was assessed by multiplying the proportion of the subzone considered capable of supporting camping (recorded in the field) by the linear distance of water bodies. This linear distance was the total perimeter of lakes in addition to two times the length of streams. In other words, it is the length of all lakeshores and streambanks, subtracting out places that are not suitable for camping, due to slopes, rockiness, etc. For some areas, a high proportion was not deemed "campable". Total weighted value per campable mile provides an aggregate campsite impact metric that should be relatively comparable across subzones that differ greatly in size and camping suitability.

To compare the two different time periods, one possibility is to compare initial conditions to conditions on those sites still being actively used as campsites in 2006 and 2007. However, this ignores all the restoration sites that have not fully recovered from camping (or they would not have been found). Also, restoration sites would have been recorded as campsites in the initial survey. So, they should be included at least in some of the impact assessments. The problem is that their condition class was not recorded. Fortunately, pictures of a substantial number of restoration sites and observations from field workers make it clear that most—but not all—of these sites would have been recorded as class 1 sites. Therefore, we decided to assign each restoration site a weighted value of 2. If 80% of restoration sites are class 1 and 20% are class 2 (a distribution likely to be close to the actual situation), this is an appropriate decision.

Most of the results report simple descriptive statistics, such as the number of sites and their condition. To assess the effect of use, environment and management on campsite condition and change, we employed t-tests, analyses of variance and regression, depending on the characteristics of the explanatory variable. We used regression when the explanatory variable has an interval scale of measurement (e.g. where elevation is measured in feet or distance to the closest trailhead is measured in miles). Where the explanatory variable has an ordinal scale of measurement and there are more than two classes (e.g. access trail type, from cross-country to unmaintained path to secondary trail to primary trail), we used analyses of variance. Where the explanatory variable has just two classes (e.g. fires allowed or prohibited), we used t-tests. Differences were considered significant where p was less than 0.05.

17

Results

Conditions in 2006-2007 are described first, followed by a description of how conditions have changed since the late 1970s. We begin with overall numbers of sites and characteristics of individual sites. Then we assess differences among subzones to explore broader scale patterns.

Campsite Conditions in 2006-2007

A total of 2,955 sites impacted by camping were located during the 2006-2007 surveys. Of these, 1,795 were considered active campsites and another 1,160 were restoration sites, apparently no longer being used for camping (Table 5). The repeat sample included 44% of the subzones originally surveyed and 45% of the campsites found in the initial survey were in these subzones. This suggests that, had the entire wilderness been surveyed, we would have found about 6600 impacted sites, of which about 4000 are being actively used as campsites.

Table 5. Number of sites impacted by camping, by condition class for sites still being used and referenced as restoration sites for those no longer being used, 2006-2007.

	Number of Sites	Percent of Campsites	Percent of All Sites
Class 1 Campsites	1084	60	37
Class 2 Campsites	549	31	19
Class 3 Campsites	134	7	5
Class 4 Campsites	28	2	1
Class 5 Campsites	0	0	0
Total Campsites	1795	100	-
Restoration Sites	1160		39
Total Impacted Sites	2955		100

Most of the campsites in the wilderness are not highly impacted. Just considering campsites and not restoration sites, 60% were rated as class 1 campsites (Table 5). Class 1 campsites range from sites that are barely noticeable (Figure 3) to sites that, although small, have clearly been trampled and have fire rings (Figure 4). Another 30% of campsites were rated as class 2 campsites. Class 2 sites are obvious campsites that do not appear highly worn (Figure 5). Only 7% of campsites were rated class 3. Class 3 sites are well-impacted popular sites, without any attributes of severe impact (Figure 6). Only 2% of campsites were rated as class 4 campsites and no campsites were rated class 5. Class 4 sites are highly-impacted, with some aspects of extreme impact. They often have large areas completely devoid of vegetation, litter and duff (Figure 7).

Figure 3. Class 1 site that is barely noticeable.

Figure 4. Class1 site with vegetation loss and a firepit.

Figure 5. Class 2 site with a substantial central area lacking vegetation.

Figure 6. Class 3 site without vegetation, litter or duff.

Figure 7. Class 4 site with widespread severe impact.

When restoration sites are considered as well, about 70 percent of sites can be considered lightly impacted (all class 1 campsites and most restoration sites). Only about 6% of sites (perhaps 350 sites in the entire wilderness) are substantially impacted (class 3 and 4 campsites) and no sites have the extreme levels of impact found on class 5 sites in the initial survey.

Number and Condition of Campsites

Of the 1160 restoration sites, 616 (53%) were judged to have been actively restored. That is, rangers had worked to eliminate evidence of use and/or keep people from camping on the site. Another 544 (47%) of the restoration sites were judged to have recovered on their own, without human assistance. Most likely, many of these sites were only used a few times. Often breaking up the fire ring removed the only evidence that anyone had ever camped there.

Appendix 1 displays the number of campsites, by condition class, and restoration sites in each subzone. It shows the large number of impacted sites in some of the more popular travel zones, such as Rae Lakes and Kearsarge Lakes. It also shows the subzones that have multiple class 4 campsites: McClure Meadow, the John Muir Trail below Center Basin, Sugarloaf Valley, Lower Rock Creek, Upper Funston and the Mid-Upper Little Five Lakes. It must be remembered, however, that the area reinventoried in 2006-2007 and included in this appendix represents just 44% of the wilderness. Such comparisons are also misleading because the subzones differ greatly in size.

Appendix 2 provides a more meaningful basis for comparing different subzones by reporting impact per unit area. Subzones with relatively high mean condition class (above 2.0) are Sphinx Creek, Sugarloaf Valley, Upper Funston, Upper Big Arroyo and Hockett Meadow. But the weighted value metrics are better indicators of aggregate impact because they are sensitive to both number of sites and condition class. Subzones with large weighted values per campable mile include Le Conte Ranger Station, the John Muir Trail below Center Basin, several areas in the Tyndall travel zone, Guitar Lake and Kern Hot Springs. Subzones that have high weighted values per hectare include McClure Meadow, the Kearsarge area, some of the Rae Lakes, Little Five Lakes and the Crabtree-Guitar Lake area. Appendix 3 ranks the subzones in order of aggregate impact, from those with the lowest weighted value per campable mile to those with the highest.

Management has encouraged visitors to camp at least 25 feet (preferably 50 feet) from water. Although 82% of campsites are located at least 50 feet from water, there are still a substantial number of sites closer to water (Table 6). Extrapolation from the sample suggests that there are still more than 250 campsites within 25 feet of water in the entire wilderness.

Table 6. Number of campsites by condition class, by distance of the campsite from water, 2006-2007.

Distance to Water				
Campsite Condition Class	0 – 25 feet	25 – 50 feet	50 – 100 feet	> 100 feet
1	80	136	228	656
2	28	74	131	323
3	6	13	36	82
4	1	2	12	16
Total	115	225	407	1077
Percent	6	12	22	59

Fortunately, most of these sites close to water are somewhat less-impacted than those further from water, perhaps reflecting less use (Figure 8). Some of the sampled subzones with a substantial number of sites still within 25 feet of water include Guitar Lake, Evolution Lake, Bench Lake, McClure Meadow, San Joaquin River and Kearsarge Lake 3 (Appendix 4).

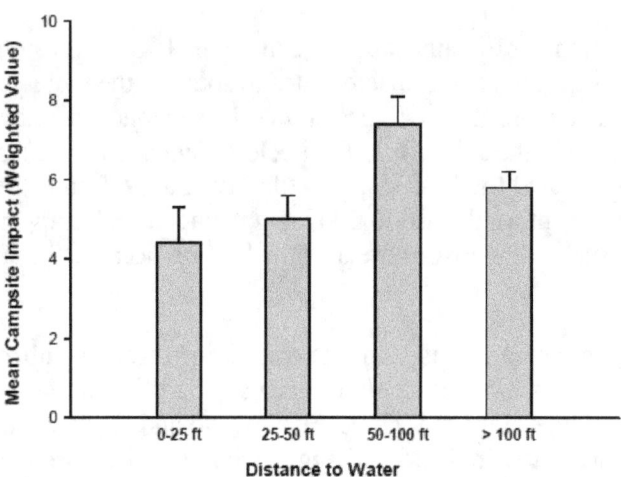

Figure 8. Variation in campsite impact with distance from water, 2006-2007 (mean weighted value and standard error).

Variation in Campsite Number and Condition

Campsites were found in a variety of vegetation types. Most campsites were in forested areas; only 13% of campsites were in the alpine zone (Table 7). An unusually large proportion of the more highly-impacted class 3 and 4 campsites were located in the montane mixed conifer forest.

Table 7. Number of campsites by condition class for different overstory types, 2006-2007.

Overstory Type										
Montane Mixed Conifer	Xeric Mixed Conifer	Red fir	Lodge-pole Pine	Lodgepole-Foxtail	Lodgepole-Whitebark	Sub-alpine Mixed Conifer	Foxtail Pine	Whitebark Pine	Open (alpine)	Other
55	35	10	376	49	157	10	17	235	145	11
41	20	13	213	21	51	3	1	101	82	10
16	9	4	56	9	9	0	0	19	12	3
7	2	1	17	1	2	0	0	0	0	1
119	66	28	662	80	219	13	18	355	239	25
7	4	2	36	4	12	1	1	20	13	1

22

In fact, there is a clear tendency for campsites in some of the mid-elevation overstory types to be more impacted than sites in higher elevation forests or above timberline (Figure 9).

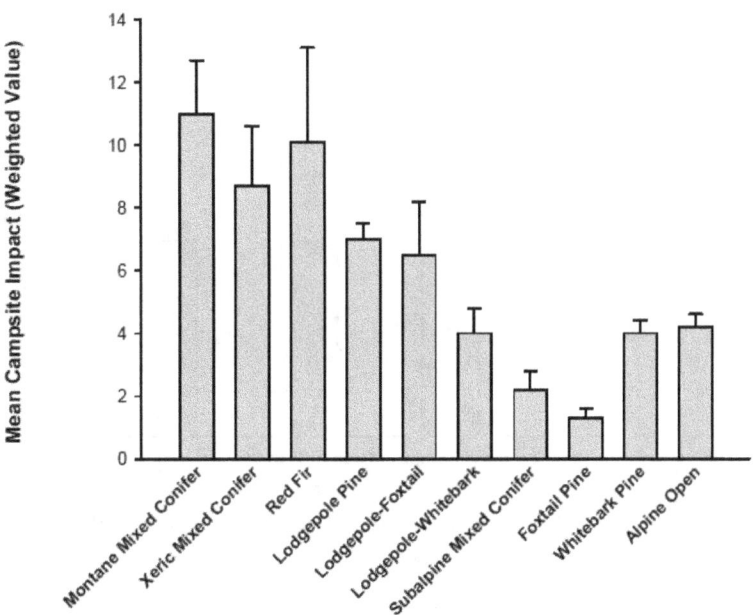

Figure 9. Differences in campsite impact between overstory types, 2006-2007 (mean weighted value and standard error).

Campsites are much more likely to be in intermediate or open forest, rather than closed forest, or within a mosaic of forest and meadow. An unusually large proportion of the more highly-impacted class 3 and 4 campsites were located in the forests with an intermediate level of canopy closure (Table 8).

Table 8. Number of campsites by condition class by degree of canopy cover for forested campsites, 2006-2007.

Forest Overstory Cover Class				
Campsite Condition Class	Open Forest	Intermediate	Closed Forest	Mosaic
1	392	284	8	260
2	111	218	6	129
3	16	67	1	38
4	3	19	1	7
Total	522	588	16	434
Percent	34	38	1	28

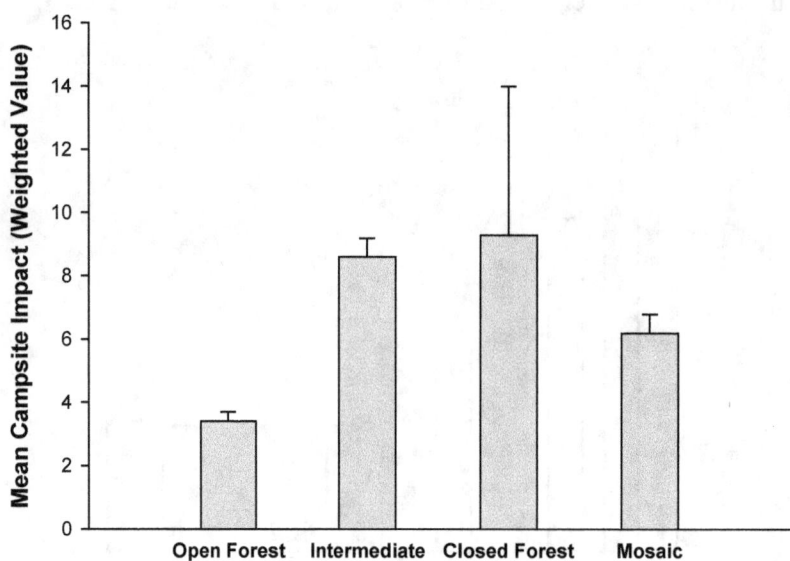

Figure 10. Differences in campsite impact between forest overstory cover classes, 2006-2007 (mean weighted value and standard error).

Consistent with this, campsites located in duff were typically more highly impacted than those with a groundcover of vegetation, rock or gravel (Figure 11).

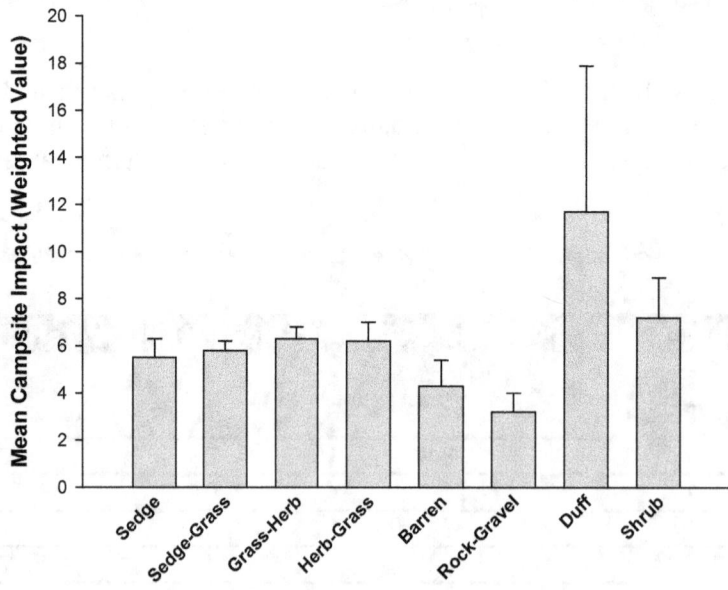

Figure 11. Differences in campsite impact between understory types, 2006-2007 (mean weighted value and standard error).

However, it is worth noting that relatively few campsites were located in duff (Table 9). Despite the fact that groundcover vegetation varies greatly in fragility (Hammitt and Cole 1998), campsite impact did not vary among the broad classes of understory vegetation that were noted.

Table 9. Number of campsites by condition class and mean site impact for different understory types, 2006-2007.

Campsite Condition Class	Understory Type							
	Sedge	Sedge-Grass	Grass-Herb	Herb-Grass	Barren	Rock and Gravel	Duff	Shrub
1	171	348	369	166	2	27	5	12
2	66	191	205	58	4	12	5	15
3	13	53	46	19	0	1	1	4
4	6	5	13	6	0	0	1	0
Total	256	597	633	249	6	40	12	31
Percent	14	33	35	14	1	2	1	2

Food storage lockers were placed in a number of popular locations in the mid-1980s, to help visitors keep their food away from bears. There are currently 82 lockers. These have concentrated use in the immediate vicinity of the lockers. Almost one-quarter of the campsites in the wilderness are located within 500 feet of a food storage locker (Table 10). This is particularly remarkable given that there are no food storage lockers in the northern half of Kings Canyon National Park.

Table 10. Number of campsites by condition class by distance of the campsite from a food storage locker, 2006-2007.

Campsite Condition Class	Distance to Food Storage Locker				
	0 – 50 feet	50 – 100 feet	100 – 250 feet	250 – 500 feet	> 500 feet
1	11	31	39	126	885
2	15	25	16	77	420
3	21	6	12	14	82
4	14	4	0	2	10
Total	61	66	67	219	1397
Percent	3	4	4	12	77

Sites in the immediate vicinity of the food storage lockers (within 50 feet) are substantially more highly-impacted than those further away (Figure 12). Some of the impact around the food storage lockers reflects the fact that lockers were typically placed in areas that were already highly impacted due to their popularity.

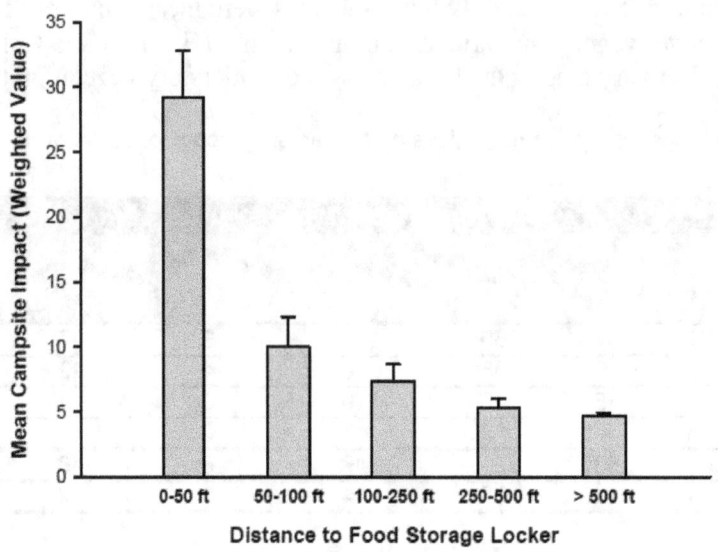

Figure 12. Variation in campsite impact with distance from food storage lockers, 2006-2007 (mean weighted value and standard error).

Less than 20% of campsites have abundant firewood or downed wood similar to undisturbed sites (Table 11). This suggests that elimination of downed woody debris, burned as firewood, is an issue even on the majority of class 1 campsites.

Table 11. Number of campsites by condition class by firewood availability class, 2006-2007. Firewood availability classes vary from 1 (very abundant, similar to undisturbed conditions) to 5 (very sparse or absent).

Campsite Condition Class	Firewood Availability Class				
	1	2	3	4	5
1	67	120	248	340	325
2	38	61	140	151	166
3	6	22	44	34	31
4	2	5	13	10	1
Total	113	208	445	535	523
Percent	6	11	24	29	29

Interestingly, the campsites with the least firewood availability are not necessarily the most impacted (Figure 13). This may result from the lack of firewood at sites above timberline.

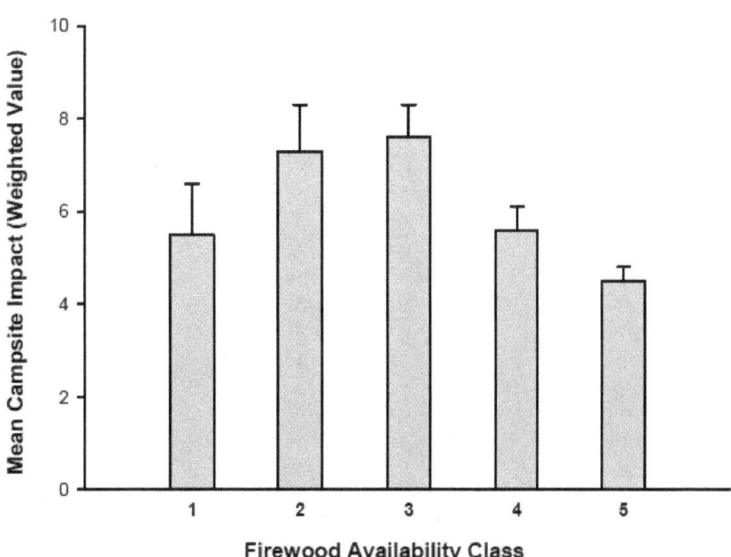

Figure 13. Variation in campsite impact with firewood availability, 2006-2007 (mean weighted value and standard error). Firewood availability classes vary from 1 (very abundant, similar to undisturbed conditions) to 5 (very sparse or absent).

When sites were surveyed, sites that had evidently been used by parties traveling with stock were noted, as was the level of impact caused by stock use. Although about 40% of sites showed some evidence of stock impact, only 2% of sites (about 70 campsites in the entire wilderness) exhibit high levels of stock impact (Table 12).

Table 12. Number of campsites by condition class on sites with various levels of evident stock impact on or around the campsite, 2006-2007.

	Firewood Availability Class				
Campsite Condition Class	1	2	3	4	5
1	67	120	248	340	325
2	38	61	140	151	166
3	6	22	44	34	31
4	2	5	13	10	1
Total	113	208	445	535	523
Percent	6	11	24	29	29

Not surprisingly, overall campsite impact is higher on sites with evidence of stock use and impact (Figure 14).

27

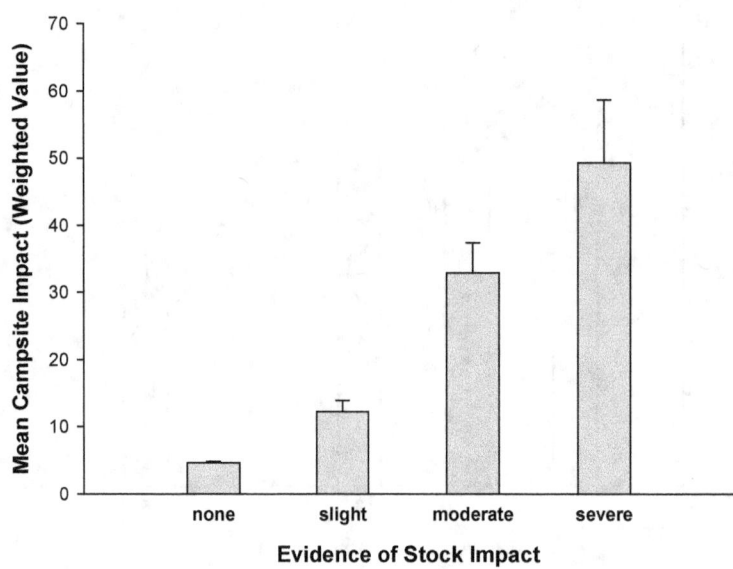

Figure 14. Variation in campsite impact with evidence of stock impact, 2006-2007 (mean weighted value and standard error).

The influence of other attributes on campsite impact can be assessed at the scale of the subzone. Given variation in the size and camping suitability of different subzones, these analyses are based on the mean weighted value per campable mile, for each subzone. Campsite impact does vary significantly with elevation zone (p = 0.03). Impact is less between 9100 and 10,900 feet than it is either below or above this elevation band (Figure 15).

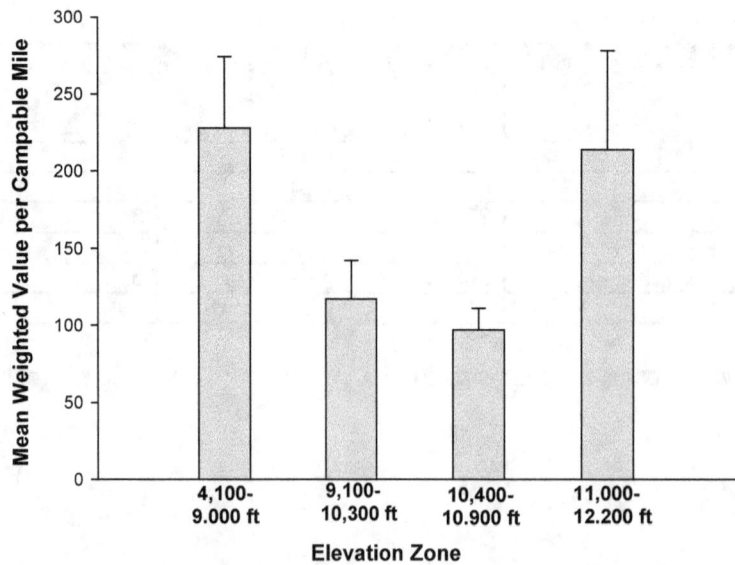

Figure 15. Variation in campsite impact with elevation zone, 2006-2007 (mean weighted value per subzone campable mile and standard error).

28

Surprisingly, campsite impact does not vary substantially with distance from the closest trailhead (Figure 16) or with distance from the closest ranger station (Figure 17).

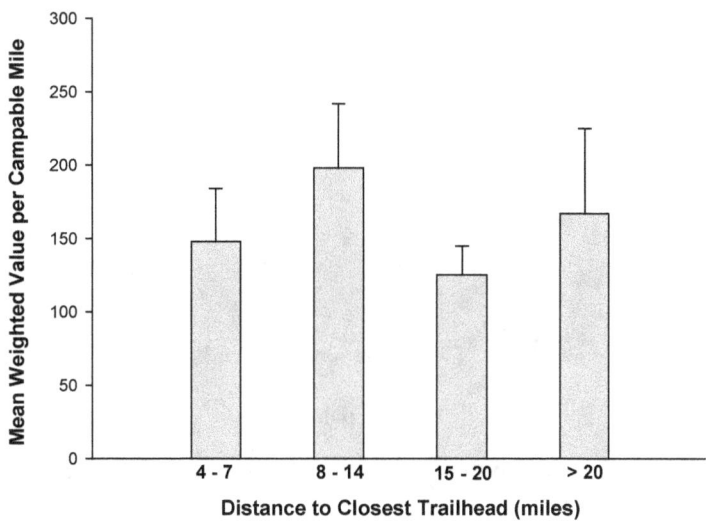

Figure 16. Variation in campsite impact with distance from the closest trailhead, 2006-2007 (mean weighted value per subzone campable mile and standard error).

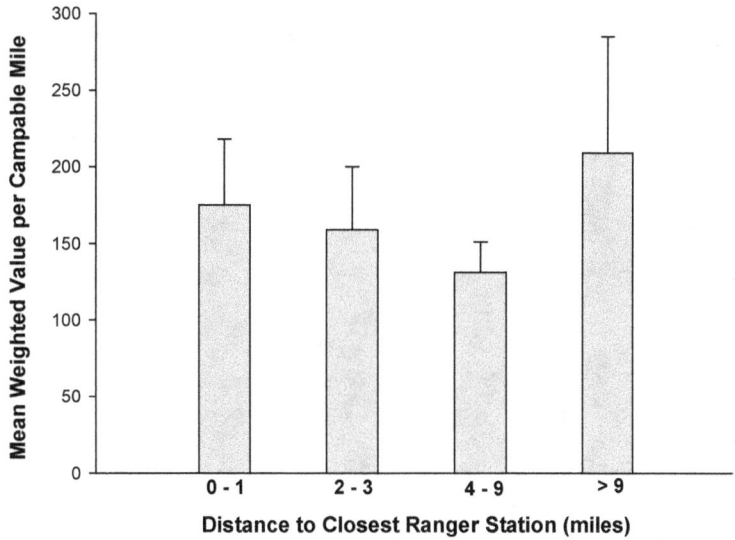

Figure 17. Variation in campsite impact with distance from the closest ranger station, 2006-2007 (mean weighted value per subzone campable mile and standard error).

The type of trail access does have an influence on campsite impact patterns. Subzones that are accessed by primary trails are more impacted than those areas accessed by secondary trails, unmaintained paths or cross-country (p = 0.03) (Figure 18).

29

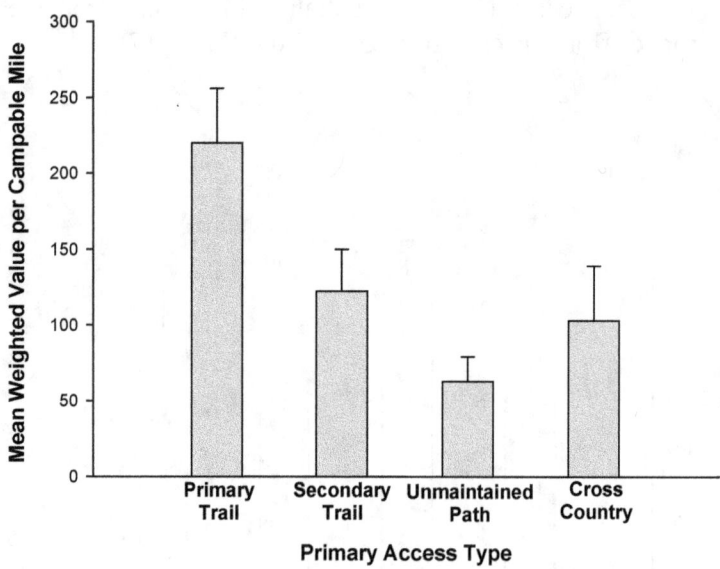

Figure 18. Variation in campsite impact with primary type of trail access, 2006-2007 (mean weighted value per subzone campable mile and standard error).

Primary trails are the John Muir Trail, High Sierra Trail, Rae Lakes Loop, Kearsarge Pass, Copper Creek, Kern River and Atwell-Hockett trails. As might be expected, campsite impact is significantly greater ($p = 0.03$) in subzones along the John Muir Trail (mean weighted value per campable mile of 227) than in other subzones (mean of 132).

Impact does not vary significantly with level of overnight stock use (Figure 19).

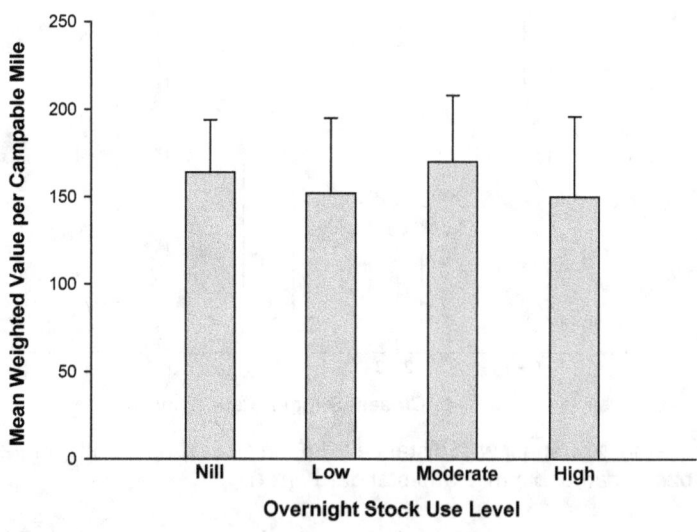

Figure 19. Variation in campsite impact with level of overnight stock use, 2006-2007 (mean weighted value per subzone campable mile and standard error).

30

Nor does it vary between subzones that allow and prohibit campfires (Figure 20).

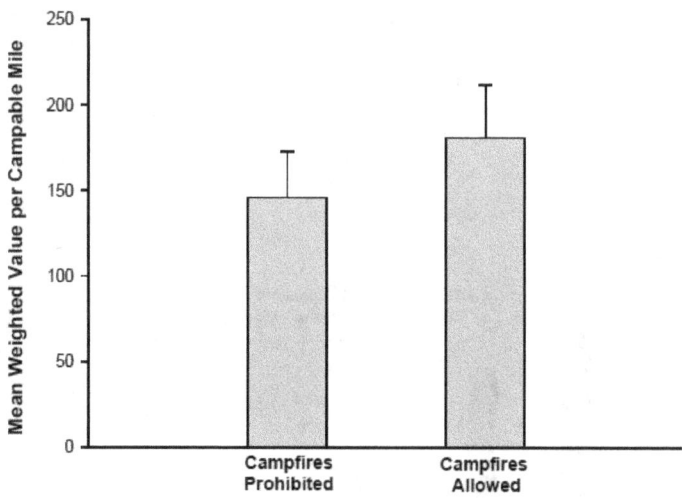

Figure 20. Variation in campsite impact with whether campfires are prohibited or allowed, 2006-2007 (mean weighted value per subzone campable mile and standard error).

Change in Campsite Conditions since the 1970s

During the 30 year period between campsite surveys, campsite impact decreased profoundly. The number of campsites decreased and the condition of remaining campsites improved (Table 13). The number of actively-used campsites in 2006-2007 was only about one-half of the number of sites that existed in the late 1970s.

Table 13. Change in the number and condition of campsites and all sites impacted by camping, in the subzones sampled in 2006-2007.

	1976-1981	2006-2007	Change	Percent Change
Class 1 campsites	1,325	1,084	-241	-18%
Class 2 campsites	1,153	549	-604	-52%
Class 3 campsites	627	134	-493	-79%
Class 4 campsites	264	28	-236	-89%
Class 5 campsites	149	0	-149	-100%
Total campsites	3,518	1,795	-1,723	-49%
Mean campsite condition class	2.08	1.50	-0.58	-28%
Weighted value, campsites	69,203	10,498	-58,705	-85%
Restoration sites	0	1,160	1,160	∞
Total sites impacted by camping	3,518	2,955	-563	-16%
Weighted value, total sites	69,203	12,818	-56,385	-81%

Even more striking, the number of class 3 sites decreased 79%; the number of class 4 sites decreased 89%; and there were no class 5 sites at the time of the repeat survey (Figure 21). The mean condition class decreased 28%. The weighted value metric, which accounts for the nonlinear nature of the condition classes and reflects both the number and condition of sites, suggests that aggregate impact on actively-used campsites decreased 85%. However, these estimates do not account for the 1160 restoration sites that still show evidence of impact from past camping. When these sites are added in, the decline in number of impacted sites is 16% (Table 13). Extrapolating the sample data to the entire wilderness, there are currently about 1250 fewer impacted sites than there were in the 1970s.

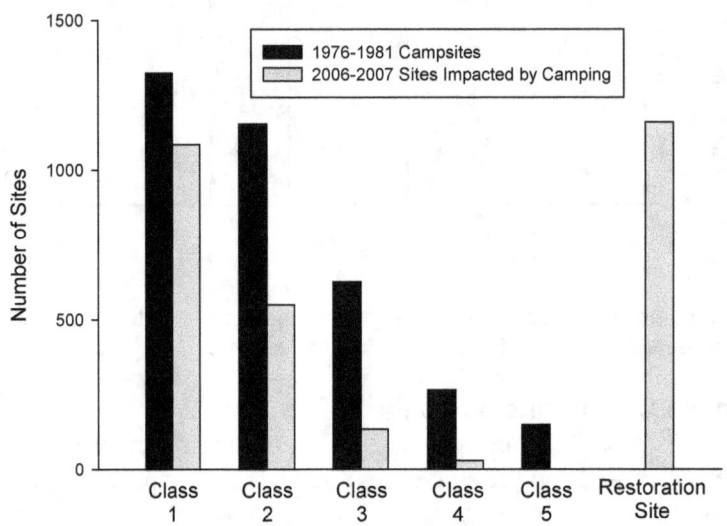

Figure 21. Change in number of sites impacted by camping, by condition class, between 1976-1981 and 2006-2007.

If we assume that 80% of these restoration sites would be rated as class 1 and the rest as class 2, the number of lightly-impacted sites actually increased over this time period (Figure 22). Nevertheless, aggregate camping impact has clearly decreased greatly. Based on the assumption above, we estimate that aggregate camping impact decreased 81% (Table 13).

Although it was not possible to assess how individual campsites changed, it is possible to assess how conditions changed in each subzone that was resurveyed in 2006-2007. Appendix 5 provides subzone-specific data for each survey period, allowing for a comparison of the number of impacted sites, mean condition class and weighted value (aggregate campsite impact). Appendix 6 lists subzones, from those that experienced the greatest proportional improvement in conditions to those that experienced the greatest proportional deterioration. Readers should note that an ordering based on absolute change, rather than proportional change, would be different. For example, did a subzone that went from having one campsite to no campsites (a 100% improvement) experience more or less change than a subzone that went from having 10 campsites to one campsite (a 90% improvement)? To allow for alternative interpretations, Appendix 6 also shows the weighted value per campable mile and per hectare, for each subzone and each time period.

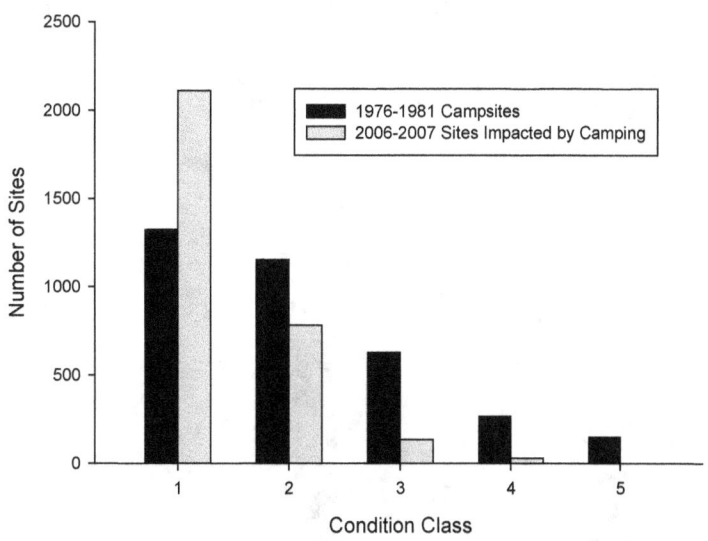

Figure 22. Change in number of sites impacted by camping, by condition class, between 1976-1981 and 2006-2007, assuming that 80% of restoration sites were class 1 sites and the rest were class 2 sites.

One of the management policies emphasized with increased vigor during the 1970s was to eliminate, to the maximum extent possible, camping close to water. Rangers attempted to obliterate campsites within 25 feet of water and, if possible, campsites within 50 feet of water. Survey data document the tremendous progress that was made. Between surveys, there was an 88% reduction in campsites within 25 feet of water and a 71% reduction in campsites 26-50 feet from water (Fig. 23).

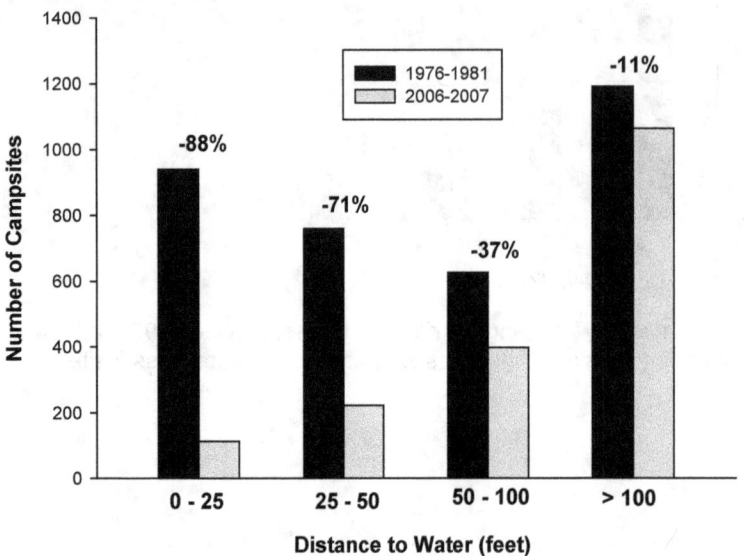

Figure 23. Change in number of campsites between 1976-1981 and 2006-2007, with distance of campsite from water. Numbers above bars are the percent change.

Variation in Campsite Number and Condition

To explore whether environmental attributes affected trends in campsite impact, we compared change in the number of impacted sites (both campsites and restoration sites) in subzones located in different elevation zones. We also compared change in the total weighted value of subzones located in different elevation zones. Decreases in both the number of impacted sites and weighted value did not differ substantially among elevation zones (Figure 24). The largest decrease in number of sites (23%) occurred at lower elevations (4,100 to 9000 feet), while the largest decrease in weighted value (84%) occurred in subzones at elevations between 10,400 and 10,900. In the 1970s, the lower elevation subzones were substantially more impacted than higher elevation subzones (based on weighted value per campable mile); this difference has become less pronounced over time (Figure 24).

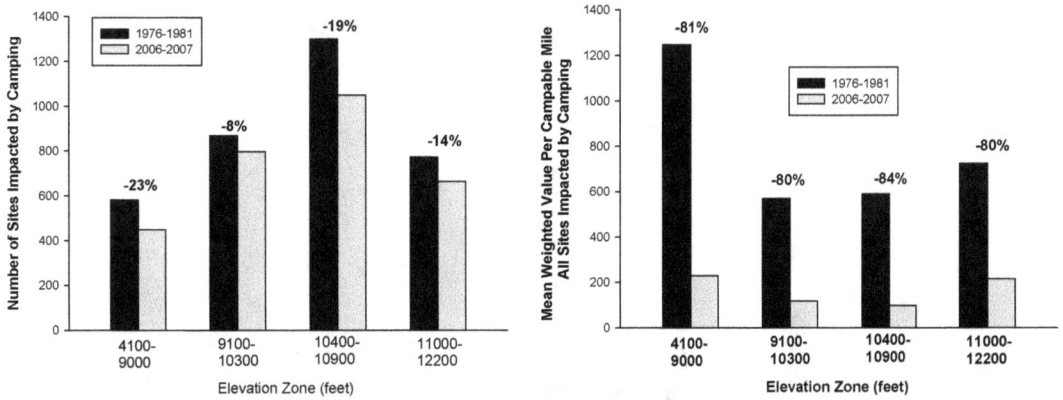

Figure 24. Change in number of sites impacted by camping and weighted value per campable mile, between 1976-1981 and 2006-2007, by elevation zone. Numbers above bars are the percent change in number of sites and in total weighted value (not weighted value per campable mile).

Amount of change varied more among vegetation types than with elevation. The largest decreases in number of sites occurred in some of the subalpine forests, particularly the subalpine mixed conifer forest, where the number of sites decreased 41% (Figure 25); in contrast, the number of sites increased 38% in open alpine vegetation. Weighted value—our measure of aggregate impact—decreased in all vegetation types (Figure 26). The largest decrease in weighted value (most improvement in conditions) occurred in subalpine mixed conifer forest (92%) and the smallest decrease occurred in open alpine vegetation (32%). In the 1970s, the most impacted subzones were those located in montane and subalpine mixed forests; more recently, the most impacted subzones are those in open alpine vegetation (Figure 26).

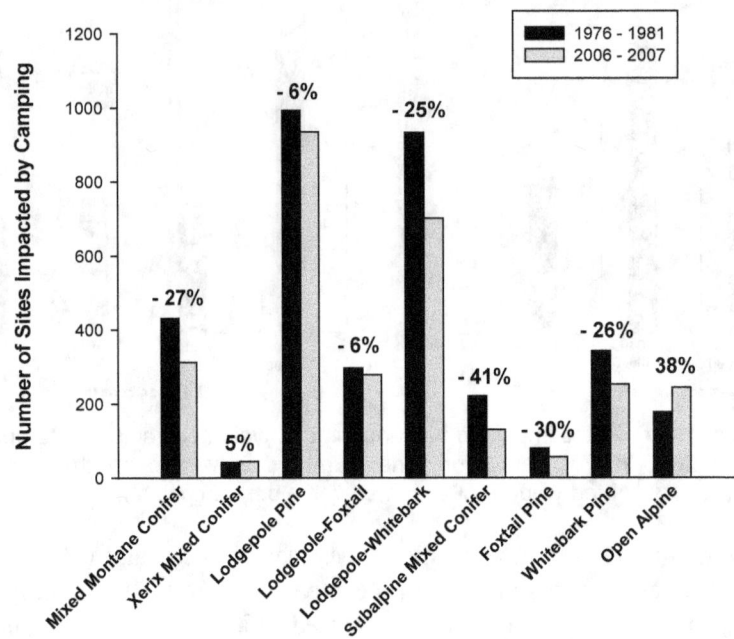

Figure 25. Change in number of sites impacted by camping between 1976-1981 and 2006-2007, by forest overstory type. Numbers above bars are the percent change in number of sites.

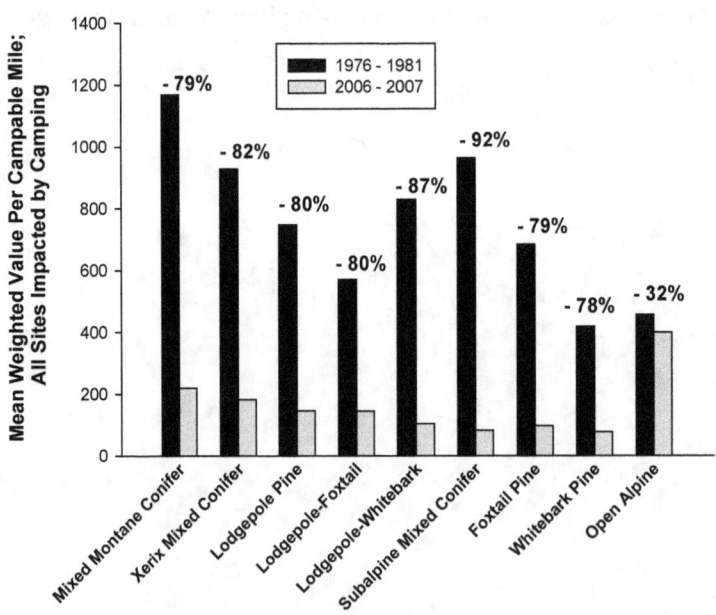

Figure 26. Change in weighted value per campable mile for all sites impacted by camping, between 1976-1981 and 2006-2007, by forest overstory type. Numbers are percent change in total weighted value (not weighted value per campable mile).

Change in the number of sites varied substantially with distance from the closest trailhead, but not in a linear fashion (Figure 27). The change in weighted value decreased with distance from the closest trailhead, suggesting there was more improvement closer to trailheads. Differences were small and not statistically significant, however. In the 1970s, subzones located closer to trailheads were substantially more impacted than those located further from trailheads. This is no longer the case (Figure 27).

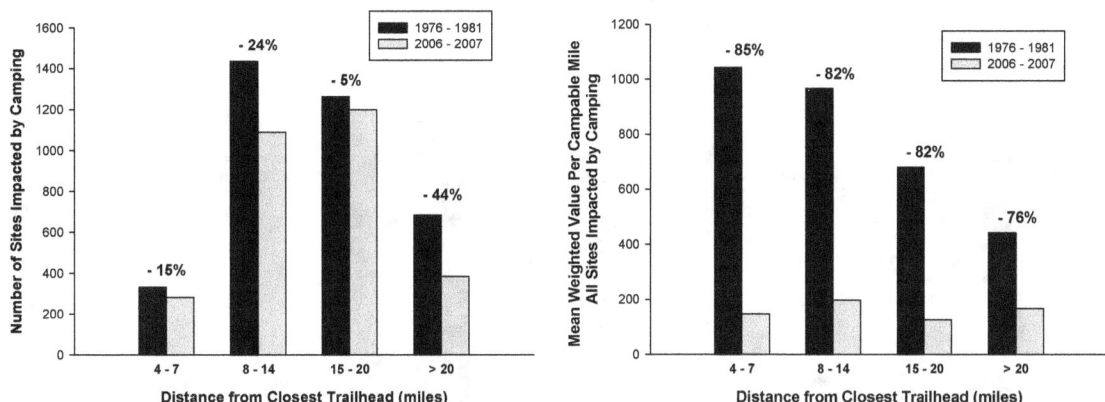

Figure 27. Change in number of sites impacted by camping and weighted value per campable mile, between 1976-1981 and 2006-2007, by distance from the closest trailhead. Numbers above bars are the percent change in number of sites and in total weighted value (not weighted value per campable mile).

A similar pattern was observed for distance to the closest ranger station. Change in number of sites was variable but not in a linear manner, while change in weighted value decreased with distance from the closest ranger station (Figure 28). In this case, the amount of improvement in conditions was significantly greater closer to ranger stations. In the 1970s, subzones located closer to ranger stations were substantially more impacted than those located further from stations. By 2006-2007, this was no longer the case (Figure 28).

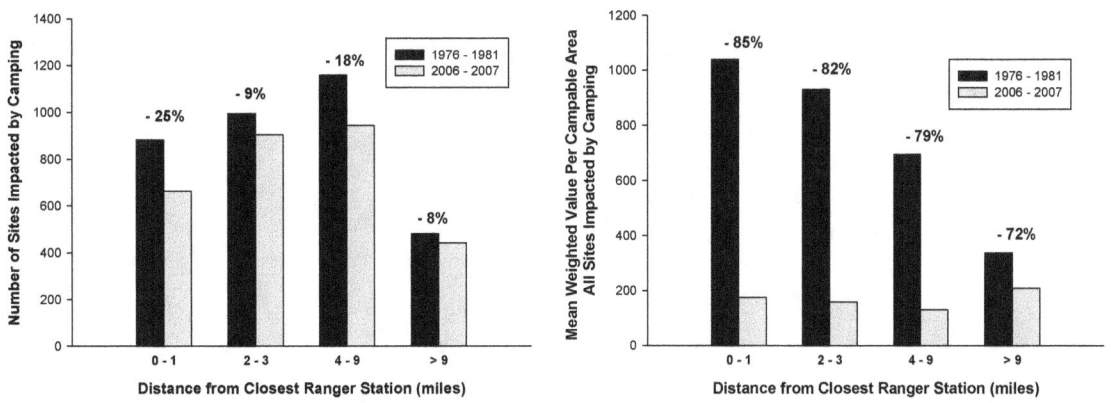

Figure 28. Change in number of sites impacted by camping and weighted value per campable mile, between 1976-1981 and 2006-2007, by distance from the closest ranger station. Numbers above bars are the percent change in number of sites and in total weighted value (not weighted value per campable mile).

Decrease in the number of sites was greatest in subzones accessed by unmaintained paths (26%) and least in cross-country subzones (7%) (Figure 29). The change in weighted value was similar in subzones accessed by primary trails, secondary trails and unmaintained paths (81-85%). It was significantly lower in cross-country subzones (56%), suggesting there has been less improvement in areas not accessed by trails and paths. In the 1970s, impact was much greater in subzones accessed by primary trails; cross-country subzones were relatively unimpacted. In 2006-2007, differences were less pronounced (Figure 29). Subzones accessed by primary trails were still most impacted but impacts in cross-country subzones were similar to those in subzones accessed by secondary trails and unmaintained paths.

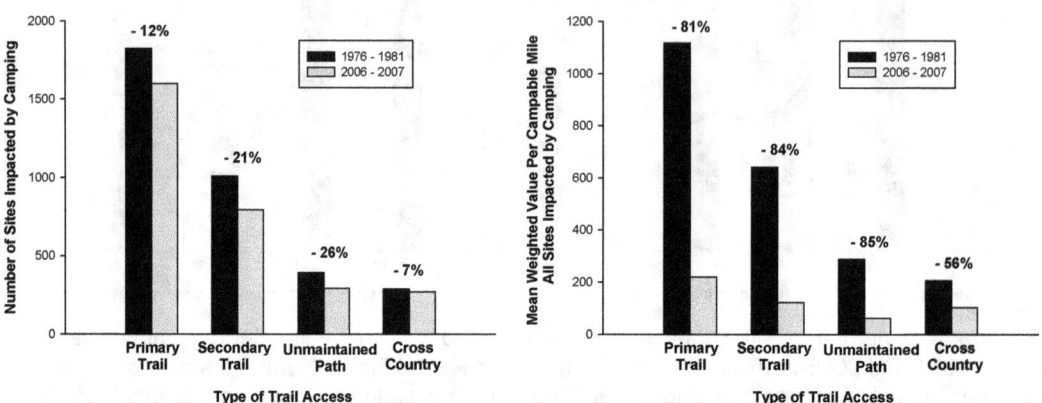

Figure 29. Change in number of sites impacted by camping and weighted value per campable mile, between 1976-1981 and 2006-2007, by type of trail access. Numbers above bars are the percent change in number of sites and in total weighted value (not weighted value per campable mile).

The number of sites decreased substantially (16-23%) in subzones with little or no overnight stock use. In subzones with moderate to high overnight stock use, the number of sites impacted by camping either did not change or increased slightly (2%) (Figure 30). However, change in weighted value did not differ significantly with level of overnight stock use. There was no consistent relationship between level of campsite impact and amount of overnight stock use, either in the 1970s or more recently (Figure 30).

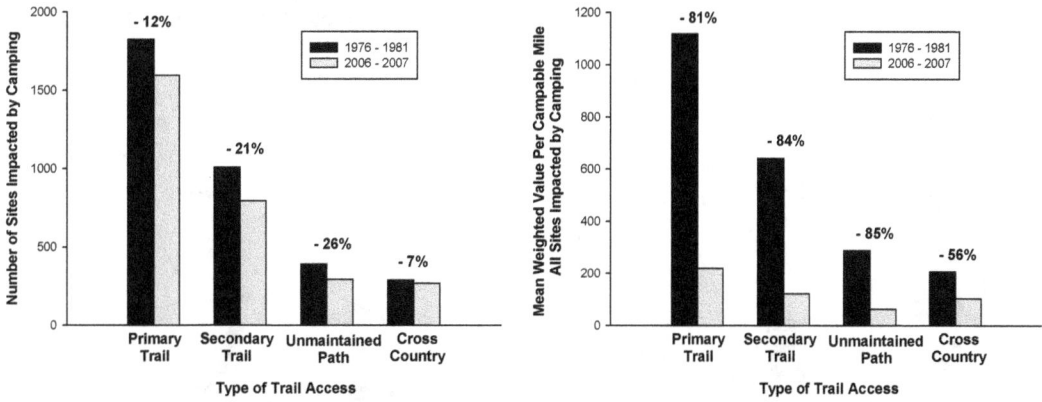

Figure 29. Change in number of sites impacted by camping and weighted value per campable mile, between 1976-1981 and 2006-2007, by type of trail access. Numbers above bars are the percent change in number of sites and in total weighted value (not weighted value per campable mile).

The number of sites decreased substantially (16-23%) in subzones with little or no overnight stock use. In subzones with moderate to high overnight stock use, the number of sites impacted by camping either did not change or increased slightly (2%) (Figure 30). However, change in weighted value did not differ significantly with level of overnight stock use. There was no consistent relationship between level of campsite impact and amount of overnight stock use, either in the 1970s or more recently (Figure 30).

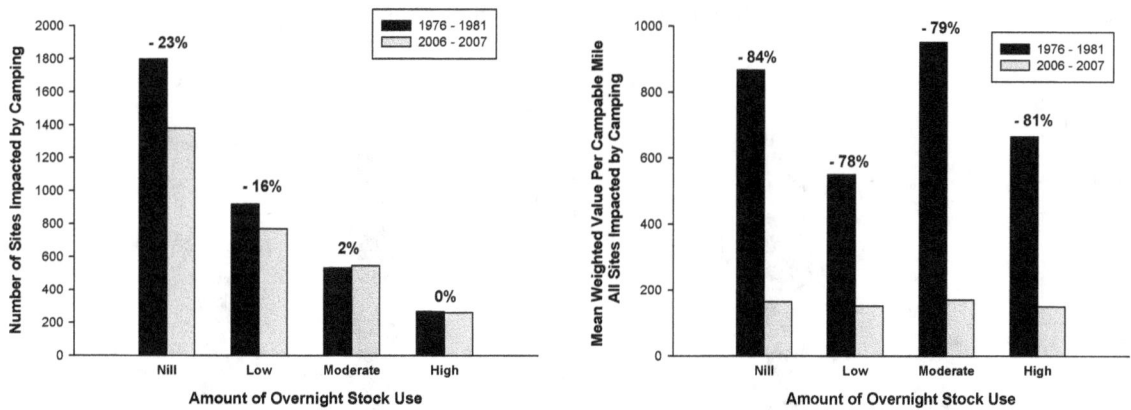

Figure 30. Change in number of sites impacted by camping and weighted value per campable mile, between 1976-1981 and 2006-2007, by amount of overnight stock use. Numbers above bars are the percent change in number of sites and in total weighted value (not weighted value per campable mile).

Whether or not campfires were allowed had little influence on change in either the number of sites or weighted value (Figure 31). This is somewhat surprising in that there is a widespread opinion that campfire restrictions have contributed significantly to the improvement in campsite conditions. There are more campsites in subzones where campfires are not allowed but mean weighted value per campable mile is greater in subzones where campfires are allowed (Figure 31), indicating that campsites are typically more impacted in subzones that allow campfires.

39

This might reflect the impacts associated with having campfires or it might reflect the amount or type of use that occurs at lower and mid-elevations or even differences in environmental durability.

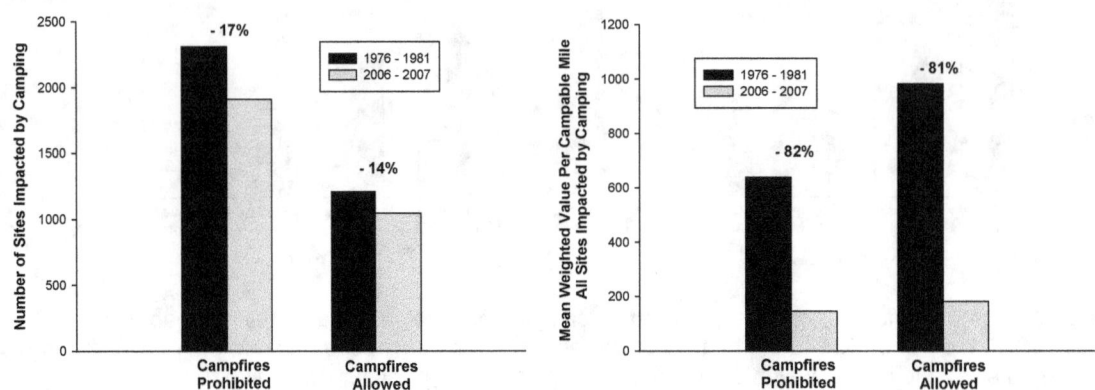

Figure 31. Change in number of sites impacted by camping and weighted value per campable mile, between 1976-1981 and 2006-2007, by whether or not campfires are allowed. Numbers above bars are the percent change in number of sites and in total weighted value (not weighted value per campable mile).

Finally, whether or not food lockers are provided also had little influence on change in either the number of sites or weighted value, at the scale of the subzone (Figure 32). This suggests that while food storage lockers may concentrate use on certain sites within subzones (see Figure 12), they do not have much effect on how use is distributed among subzones.

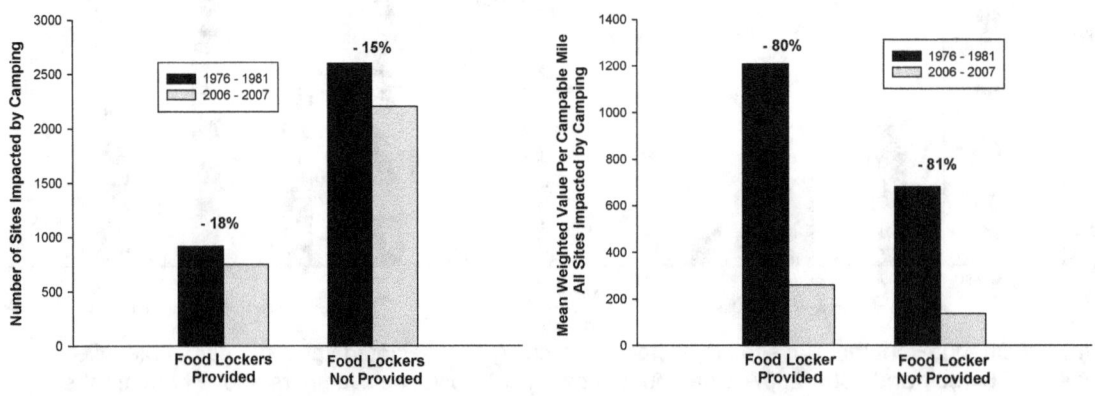

Figure 32. Change in number of sites impacted by camping and weighted value per campable mile, between 1976-1981 and 2006-2007, by whether or not food lockers are provided. Numbers above bars are the percent change in number of sites and in total weighted value (not weighted value per campable mile).

This finding suggests that the oft-observed concentration of use and impact around food lockers is highly localized, with little meaningful effect on either the number of campsites or aggregate campsite impact at larger scales. There are more campsites in subzones where food lockers are

40

not provided but mean weighted value per campable mile is greater in subzones where food lockers are provided (Fig. 32), indicating that campsites are typically more impacted in subzones that provide food lockers. This likely reflects the fact that lockers were located in highly impacted places as much as the tendency for food lockers to concentrate use and impact.

Why Some Subzones Improved More Than Others

The preceding discussion suggests that the greatest improvement in conditions occurred on campsites close to water and in places that were close to ranger stations, with good trail access, without much overnight stock use and in some of the upper subalpine forests. Substantially less improvement occurred in remote cross-country locations above timberline. While this conclusion is correct it misses the more fundamental observation that the places that improved the most were the places that were most highly impacted in the past. A simple regression model with change in weighted value as the dependent variable and weighted value at the time of the initial survey had an r^2 of 0.98 (Table 14). That is 98% of the variation among subzones in how much change occurred is explained by the initial amount of impact. The places that were most impacted originally improved the most, while those that were least impacted changed the least. Once this source of variation is accounted for, factors such as elevation, vegetation type, trail access, distance to the nearest trailhead and distance to the nearest ranger station no longer have any significant effect. Level of overnight stock use has a statistically significant but minor effect. This result was explored further by testing whether or not residuals (the degree to which a subzone improved more or less than would be predicted by its initial level of impact) varied significantly with environmental, locational or managerial factors associated with each subzone. Residuals did not vary significantly with elevation, vegetation type, type of trail access, distance to trailhead or ranger station, amount of overnight stock use or campfire restrictions.

Table 14. Multiple regression results for variables that influence change in total campsite impact (weighted value).

Model	Source	df	MS	F	R	Adjusted R^2
1	Regression	1	28390658	4529*	0.98	0.98
	Residual	118	6269			
2	Regression	2	14207346	2322*	0.98	0.98
	Residual	117	6117			

Model	Variables entered	Unstandardized Coefficients	Beta Coefficients	t value
1	Weighted value; 1976-1981	- 0.88	-0.99	-67.29*
2	Weighted value; 1976-1981	- 0.88	- 0.99	-67.29*
	Level of stock use	14.67	0.03	1.98*

* $P < 0.05$

Variables that did not enter the equation at the $p = 0.05$ significance level: elevation, distance to the nearest trailhead, distance to the nearest ranger station, and access trail type.

The ten subzones with residuals lower than -1.0 (those that most improved beyond predictions) are all along or close to the John Muir Trail: Charlotte Lake, McGee Lakes, Grouse Meadow, Kearsarge Lake 3, Upper 60 Lakes, Rae Lake 3, Crabtree Ranger Station, Lower Kearsarge Lake, South Rae Lake 2 and Upper Whitney Creek (Figure 33). The eleven subzones with residuals higher than 1.0 (those that improved least compared to predictions) are more diverse in situation. The two subzones with the highest residuals, Guitar Lake and the John Muir Trail below Center Basin, are both on the John Muir Trail, as are Evolution Lake and McClure

41

Meadow. Like Guitar Lake, Lower Rock Creek is on a popular route to climb Mt. Whitney. Other subzones with high residuals are Upper Big Arroyo, Upper Funston, McClure Meadow, Kern Hot Springs, Mid-Upper Little Five Lakes, Panther-Alta and Sugarloaf Valley.

The story of campsite impact distribution and change seems to be that, as wilderness use increased in the parks, the most severe campsite impacts developed within spectacular subalpine lake basins, along primary trails—places like Charlotte Lake, Rae Lakes, Kearsarge Lakes, Guitar Lake and Soldier Lake. These places were at variable distances from trailheads. At many of these popular destinations, existing structures were adapted to serve as ranger stations. These were not places characterized recently by heavy overnight stock use, because forage is often limited. These same places that were initially so highly impacted are the places where conditions have improved the most since the 1970s. Although many of these places are still among the places most impacted by camping, they are in much better condition than they were in the 1970s. The difference among subzones, in magnitude of impact, has decreased over the past three decades.

Original and repeat maps of each subzone provide a way to assess change in conditions in detail. Three maps were produced for each subzone. One map shows campsites, classified by condition class, as well as restoration sites in 2006-2007. For the 1970s data, two maps were done. One shows the campsites on the same base map used for the 2006-2007 data. However, there is no way to gauge condition class from this map. Therefore, we also reproduced a map developed in the 1970s, where dots were placed on a topographic map, with the size of the dot increasing in size as campsite impact increased. It is important to remember that these campsites were not located using Global Positioning System (GPS) technology. They were located based on proximity to features included on the topographic maps, such as trails and drainages—attributes that may be inaccurate on the topographic map or that can change in location over time. This makes it impossible to compare individual sites between the two sampling periods. There are too many maps to provide all of them in this publication, but examples from two subzones are provided in Appendix 8.

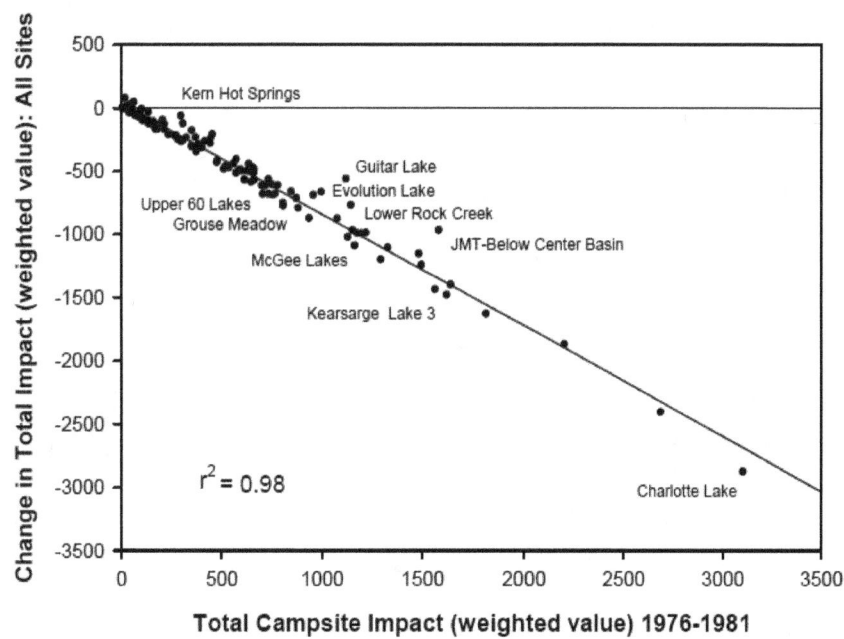

Figure 33. Scatterplot relating change in campsite impact to initial campsite impact for each subzone. Negative values for change indicate less impact in 2006-2007. Named subzones are those that deviated most from the regression line--five that improved more than predicted (below the diagonal line) and five that improved less than expected (above the diagonal line).

Study Limitations

Our estimate of the magnitude of change in campsite condition is subject to at least four potential sources of error. First, it is dependent on the weights assigned to each condition class. However, even if the weights were all decreased by 50% (so that a class 2 site is three times as impacted as a class 1 site and a class 5 site is seventy-five times as impacted as a class 1 site), the effect on our estimate of change would be minor. With this change in weighting, our estimate would be a 79% improvement rather than an 81% improvement. Based on this lack of sensitivity and our belief that the weights still seem reasonable, we conclude that this is not a significant source of error.

The other three sources of error reflect the comparability of the reinventory. First is the issue of not recording the condition class of sites considered to be restoration sites rather than active campsites. Our assumption that 80% of these sites would have been given a rating of class 1, with the rest assigned to class 2, seems reasonable. Field visits and examination of photographs indicate that the vast majority of restoration sites are class 1 and none appear to be higher than class 2. However, if restoration sites are more highly impacted, our estimate of improvement may be slightly too high. A second issue is the comparability of search behavior. On this account, the reinventory appears to have been slightly more thorough than the initial inventory. There are clearly a few places (portions of 7 different subzones) that were missed in the initial inventory and our field checks suggest that search behavior was very thorough during the reinventory. Given this, our estimate of improvement may be slightly too low. Again, we conclude that these sources of error are negligible.

The only source of error that we believe might have had a substantial effect on our estimate of change is the degree to which different evaluators made similar judgments about campsite condition. Every effort was made to ensure comparability, by investing substantially in training and in spending field time with one of the people involved in the 1970s inventory. The authors of this report also took two field trips, in an attempt to assess the comparability of condition class judgments. One of us conceived and oversaw the original inventory (DJP) and the other has extensive experience with campsite condition assessments elsewhere (DNC). First, it is important to be clear that it is not possible to objectively test the degree to which repeat evaluations were consistent with original evaluations and that park employees went to great lengths to ensure comparability. That said, it is our opinion that condition class ratings from the 2006-2007 inventory were somewhat lower than ratings given in the 1970s. For example, in the 1970s inventory, class 1 sites were "usually no more than a small sleep site and possibly a small fire ring with little or no sign of trampling or vegetation impact" (Parsons and Stohlgren 1987, p. 14). Some of the campsites rated class 1 in the 2006-2007 inventory had experienced long-lasting impact, including substantial disturbance of vegetation and duff (Figure 4). If our opinion is correct—and there is no way to be sure—this does not change the overall conclusions of this report. It would only change our quantitative estimate of the magnitude of improvement.

In an attempt to provide a more conservative magnitude of improvement, assume that one-half of the campsites were assigned a condition rating one class lower than in the 1970s inventory. We cannot imagine the discrepancy between the two evaluations being larger than this. Even with this adjustment, the number of class 3, 4 and 5 sites decreased by 46%, 69% and 91%, respectively, over the past 30 years. Based on weighted value, aggregate campsite impact has

45

decreased 62% since the 1970s. While this magnitude of improvement is less than the 81% improvement estimate based on the 2006-2007 inventory ratings, it does not change the overall conclusion of this report. Campsite conditions have improved profoundly since the 1970s, with aggregate campsite impact decreasing somewhere between 60 and 80%, depending upon assumptions and the comparability of the inventories.

Discussion and Management Implications

The most important finding of this study is that campsite conditions in the wilderness of Sequoia and Kings Canyon National Parks have improved dramatically since the late 1970s. Depending on assumptions and the comparability of the two surveys, aggregate campsite impact in 2006-2007 is almost certainly less than one-third what it was in the 1970s. The initial campsite survey was conducted because campsite impacts were proliferating and there was a widespread fear that impacts would continue to increase. While there might have been hope that active wilderness management might reverse this trend, the magnitude of improvement that has occurred is remarkable, particularly in relation to what has been observed in other wildernesses.

There have been relatively few other studies of trends in campsite condition and findings from those studies have been highly variable. Some studies have found increasing campsite impacts over time. This was the case in three wildernesses in Oregon and Montana (Eagle Cap, Selway-Bitterroot and Lee Metcalf) with little management presence and where visitors are allowed to camp wherever they want (Cole 1993); however, it was also the case in Grand Canyon National Park where there is substantial management presence and where camping is confined to designated sites in some wilderness zones (Cole et al. 2008). In portions of two Oregon wildernesses (Three Sisters and Mount Jefferson), campsite conditions were little changed four years after implementation of a designated campsite policy (Hall 2001). Studies in two eastern parks (Delaware Water Gap and Shenandoah), conversely, have documented successful reductions in campsite impact following implementation of a regulation requiring people to camp on designated campsites (Marion 1995, Reid and Marion 2004). Finally, in Caney Creek Wilderness, Arkansas, an active program of trail location, education, closure of selected campsites and site restoration resulted in a substantial improvement in campsite conditions without requiring the use of designated campsites (Cole and Ferguson 2009). This management approach and result is most similar to what was observed at Sequoia and Kings Canyon National Parks; however, the magnitude of improvement was not nearly as dramatic as at Sequoia and Kings Canyon.

The second fundamental finding of this study is that the improvement in conditions that has occurred over the past 30 years has been remarkably uniform. Virtually without exception, conditions have improved throughout the wilderness of Sequoia and Kings Canyon National Parks. When the repeat survey was initiated, the primary question of interest—beyond how conditions have changed since the 1970s—was what factors have influenced the patterns of change that have occurred? That is, have some places changed much more, or in different ways, than others and, if so, why? Visitor use, management activity and site fragility are all spatially variable. Consequently, it is reasonable to expect that some places—perhaps those most heavily used and most fragile—would deteriorate more than others. Many people felt, for example, that the placement of food storage lockers at select locations would increase impact nearby. Or alternatively, some expressed concern that near-pristine portions of the wilderness might disappear because they are particularly vulnerable to degradation (Cole 1993). Since a given increment of use causes most impact when it occurs where there has been little prior use (Hammitt and Cole 1998), even slight increases in the use of previously unused places could result in substantial deterioration. Questions that were asked when the reinventory was initiated included, are impacts spreading more than intensifying? Is near-pristine wilderness slowly disappearing?

The answers to these questions are surprisingly simple. Impacts are not spreading or intensifying; they have retreated and diminished in magnitude. Near-pristine wilderness is not disappearing; it may be expanding. The food storage lockers may have intensified use on a few sites in the immediate vicinity. But they were placed on sites that were already highly impacted. Given increased use of minimum impact techniques, including Leave-No-Trace (Leave No Trace n.d.), these sites are often in better condition now than they were in the past, even if use intensity has increased. Food storage lockers have had no apparent effect on campsite impact at the scale of the subzone.

Campsite impacts are not equitably distributed. They are more substantial along primary trails, particularly the John Muir Trail, and they are concentrated both in particularly popular subzones (e.g. the Rae Lakes) and within subzones, at trail junctions, creek crossings and along lakeshores. However, because the most highly impacted places are the ones that have improved most, the disparity between more and less impacted places has decreased. In the 1970s, campsite impact decreased significantly with increases in elevation, distance from the trailhead and distance from the closest ranger station. Campsite impact no longer varies with any of these factors.

Why Have Conditions Improved So Much?

There are several competing potential explanations for the decrease in campsite impact over the past 30 years. There is evidence that use levels are not as high today as they were in the 1970s. There is also evidence that use is more concentrated in space than it was in the 1970s. Although the relationship between impact and the spatial distribution of use is complex, impacts are most often less pronounced in areas where use is concentrated rather than more widely distributed (Hammitt and Cole 1998). Visitor behavior has also changed. There has been widespread adoption of Leave-No-Trace techniques and some of the activities with high impact potential (e.g. campfire building and traveling with larger packstock groups) are more tightly regulated. Finally, conditions might have improved as a result of management actions taken to reduce campsite impacts.

It is our contention that all of these factors have contributed to improvement in conditions and that they are often synergistic in their effect. However, campsite conditions have not improved as much in other wildernesses that have experienced declining use, more concentrated use and widespread adoption of Leave-No-Trace techniques. The most distinctive aspect of the situation at Sequoia and Kings Canyon is the investment in a relatively large cadre of highly-experienced wilderness rangers that remain in the field throughout the summer season. Consequently, we believe that **the primary reason for success has been the concerted effort and hard work of wilderness rangers to reduce campsite impact throughout the wilderness, guided by approaches developed by wilderness management staff**. Below, we explain how we arrived at this conclusion.

Amount of Use

Everything else being equal, impact should increase as amount of use increases and use statistics indicate that, in 2006-2007, overnight use (visitor use nights) of Sequoia and Kings Canyon Wilderness was only about 50% of peak use in the 1970s. However, it is a challenge to obtain accurate use estimates, particularly where entry points are on lands administered by other agencies, and reporting procedures have changed over the years. Carefully examining the trends evident in the data presented in Figure 1 it appears that (1) use increased dramatically prior to

1974, (2) use declined somewhat between 1974 and 1994, (3) use plummeted 50% in just one year, between 1994 and 1995 and (4) use has increased somewhat since 1995. The unprecedented 50% decrease in use between 1994 and 1995 is troubling. It accounts for more than 90% of the difference in use between 1974 and 2010. More important, the 1995 use level was not just a temporary drop in use. It established a new baseline, at a use level substantially below levels reported in 1994 and before. This is more suggestive of a change in counting or statistical reporting procedures than in amount of use. Anecdotal evidence, including ranger observations, suggests that there is less use than there was at the height of the backpacking boom of the 1970s; there is widespread agreement about this. However, the magnitude of decline is probably not as great as is suggested by the use estimates presented in Figure 1.

The decline in use by groups with packstock has been even more dramatic than the decline in overall use. Since the 1980s, the annual number of stock use nights for all types of use (administrative, commercial and private) has declined almost 30% and private stock use has declined almost 60%.

Reductions in use levels do not necessarily result in reduced impact. Once impacted, a high degree of campsite impact can be sustained by relatively low levels of ongoing use. This is particularly true at higher elevations where recovery rates are low (Stohlgren and Parsons 1986, Hammitt and Cole 1998). Reductions in use can lead to reductions in impact if visitors camp on fewer sites. But this requires management action, such as a designated campsite policy or action by rangers to reduce the number of sites. In other words, reductions in use can supplement the effectiveness of management actions and the efforts of rangers to reduce the number of campsites; but the primary reason for improvement is management action and ranger effort.

Distribution of Use

During the 1970s, trips that followed unmaintained paths and cross-country routes increased in popularity. Guidebooks were published advertising these paths and routes and more people seemed inclined to put the effort into visiting more pristine places in the wilderness. This was a change from the period prior to the 1970s and is a change that seems to have reversed in recent decades. As was mentioned earlier, the distribution of use among trailheads and among travel zones is slightly more concentrated today than it was in the 1970s. Wilderness travel has become increasingly goal-oriented; there is much less wandering about or going to one favorite place for an extended stay. Interest in climbing Mount Whitney (and to a lesser extent other mountains over 14,000 feet) or hiking the entire John Muir Trail has skyrocketed. The number of people hiking the entire John Muir Trail has increased six-fold since 1998 to where, by some estimates, these hikers may constitute as much as 10% of total wilderness use. In contrast, rangers and other experienced observers think that cross-country travel has declined greatly. There has been a particular decrease in the use of places with less spectacular or iconic scenery. Consequently, use is more concentrated than it was in the 1970s.

Use concentration has also been the unintended consequence of a number of management actions. Variable trail budgets and shifting trail maintenance priorities may have concentrated use on a smaller network of trails. Fish stocking into naturally fishless high-elevation lakes was terminated in 1987-1988, which led to the gradual disappearance of fish from water bodies in which they could not reproduce, but leaving almost 600 reproducing populations. More recently, in order to restore native frog populations, fish have been removed from about two dozen lakes.

These actions collectively may have diverted fishermen from a few lake basins and redirected them elsewhere

Campfire prohibitions have sometimes pushed use by those interested in having a campfire down to lower elevations. Camping use is often concentrated just below the lower limit of the no-fire zone. Moreover, as these limits have been lowered, use patterns have shifted. For example, when campfires were allowed, visitors staging a climb of Mount Whitney from the west would often camp among the highest trees; today they cannot have a campfire anywhere within an easy day of the Whitney summit. So, large numbers of people have started camping along drainages above Guitar Lake, one of the few places that is more highly impacted now than it was in the 1970s. The provision of food storage lockers in select locations has concentrated use, as have restrictions on where packstock can travel and graze. Camping is also confined to designated sites in a few places, none of which were reinventoried.

If use has become more concentrated, there is less impetus for making new campsites and many of the campsites of the 1970s must be used much less frequently today. Sites that are being used more often tend to be in popular places that are already highly impacted; increased use is unlikely to damage them further. Consequently, aggregate impact should be reduced. However, as noted before, even infrequent use is often sufficient to limit campsite recovery. Therefore, without active closure and restoration of campsites, increasingly concentrated use is not likely to cause a rapid reduction in impact. As was the case with reductions in amount of use, use concentration supplements the effectiveness of site management efforts by the wilderness rangers.

Visitor Behavior

Regulations have curtailed some of the more high-impact camping behaviors. In particular, campfires are now prohibited in more than one-half of the subzones that were reinventoried. As a result, campsites are less developed and there is less impetus for damaging trees. Group size limits have been reduced, so there is less need for very large campsites. Packstock groups are more tightly controlled. More importantly, most visitors have become aware of the adverse impacts they can cause if they behave inappropriately and have voluntarily adopted Leave-No-Trace behaviors. This change in behavior is most reflected in the relative lack of litter and lack of campsite developments (e.g. tables, chairs, etc.). Tree damage also seems much less problematic than in the past. Many visitors avoid camping on vegetation and they have learned that their impact can often be minimized by camping in places that are already highly impacted.

These behavioral changes have probably contributed much more to improvement of conditions than changes in either the amount or distribution of use. However, there are still some visitors who have campfires where they are prohibited and who resist adopting Leave-No-Trace behaviors. Unfortunately, substantial impact can be caused by even a small minority of users unless rangers can constantly be vigilant about dealing with newly-created impacts and maintaining camping conditions that encourage low impact behaviors. Visitors to wildernesses that have experienced increases in campsite impact have also adopted Leave-No-Trace techniques. Lack of improvement there is likely more reflective of the degree of management presence than the ethic of the majority of visitors.

Campsite Management Implemented By Wilderness Rangers

Although campsites were managed before the initial campsite survey, park management adopted a greater sense of urgency regarding reducing campsite impact and developed a more consistent and aggressive management strategy. The fundamental strategy that evolved over time involved concentrating use on a smaller number of campsites, in appropriate locations, working to reduce campsite size and development, more actively maintaining campsites and educating visitors. Specific actions taken to implement this strategy included:

- obliterating unnecessary campsites when there are plenty of others around,
- eliminating sites too close to water, particularly those within 25 feet,
- eliminating campsite developments, such as built up tables, rock walls, etc.
- building small fire rings (often 3 rocks set in the ground) at certain campsites and maintaining them,
- reducing the size of very large sites,
- constantly eliminating campfire evidence where fires are illegal, and
- educating visitors about how to minimize their impact.

If these actions had not been taken, campsite conditions would probably have improved very little, despite reductions in use levels, changes in use distribution and improved visitor behavior.

The scope and magnitude of this effort was gleaned from interviews with long-time wilderness rangers, end-of-season ranger station logs and other documents. In 1981, the Rae Lakes ranger reported eliminating or rehabilitating 847 fire rings in the area between Mather Pass and Forester Pass. The number of sites removed or cleaned up by the Rae Lakes ranger was 132 in 1982, 108 in 1983, 66 in 1984, 78 in 1986, 100 in 1987, and 168 in 1988. This would have dramatically reduced the number of campsites in that area and reduced impacts on those sites that remained. The ranger commented on the hard work required, as it was necessary to remove rocks, any ash and trash and then to cover the area with clean soil and that ongoing maintenance is required. However, once the initial work is done, subsequent work is easier. As an example, the Rae Lakes ranger described removing 45 fire rings at Bench Lake in 1982, many of which were quite large. Three weeks later, seven new fire rings had appeared, but they were small and easy to remove.

In 1988, rangers kept careful track of their campsite removal and maintenance efforts. Across the entire wilderness, they eliminated 206 campsites and 1014 fire sites. In addition, they cleaned up another 88 campsites and another 348 fire sites. Let's assume that this level of effort is reflective of efforts today on the approximately 4000 active campsites in the wilderness. This would mean that rangers are annually working to eliminate about 5% of campsites and about 25% of fire sites. They are diligently maintaining conditions on more than 10% of sites, probably those that are most frequently used. The most common reason for doing this work was fire sites located in areas where wood fires are prohibited. This was the case for 569 of the fire sites that were eliminated. Other reasons for action were campsites within 25 feet of water (225 sites), overly large sites (299 sites), and either multiple fire rings on individual sites or more sites than necessary in a particular location (218 sites).

As these numbers attest, substantial effort goes into limiting campsite impact and maintaining campsite conditions. Fire rings have to be removed when people build fires in places where fires are not allowed or on sites where there is no established fire ring. Campsites need to be removed

51

when established too close to water, in other sensitive locations, or in areas where there are already enough other campsites. Developments occasionally need to be dismantled; rock walls built as wind breaks at high elevation sites may be the most common example these days. Where fires are allowed, fire rings need to be maintained, as frequently as every two weeks in popular places. Rangers also attempt to keep campsite size from expanding and to keep use and campfires concentrated on sites where such use will not cause further impact.

Recommendations

1. Continue to support the field wilderness ranger program and keep doing what you are doing. This is the obvious conclusion that follows from finding such an unprecedented, unexpected and ubiquitous improvement in conditions over the past 30 years and our conclusion that improvement is mostly reflective of the campsite management program carried out by the wilderness rangers. Continue to concentrate camping and campfires, to eliminate campsites in sensitive locations or where they are unnecessary, to maintain campsites and fire sites in popular locations and to educate visitors on minimum impact practices.

2. Continue to visit with the wilderness rangers about management actions that might improve conditions. We heard a number of suggestions in our interviews. Some are general, such as the desirability of a smaller group size limit (e.g. 8 people) when traveling off-trail. Others are more site-specific. For example, several people noted ongoing impact problems at Woods Creek Crossing that need addressing. The change to Rae Lakes regulations, allowing a 2-night stay, was raised as an example of an action that has increased impacts. It should also be noted that whenever there are changes in wood fire restrictions or in food storage locker locations, changes in campsite condition follow.

3. Complete the reinventory of campsites. Only 44% of the wilderness was reinventoried in 2006 and 2007. For subzones not reinventoried, it is important to establish a more recent inventory of conditions than the 1970s data provides. In addition, the inventory of sites is extremely helpful to the rangers in their program of campsite management and maintenance. Before moving forward with more campsite monitoring work, the parks should consider changing monitoring procedures. Concerns about existing procedures and some possible alternatives are discussed in Appendix 7.

4. Document the administrative history of wilderness management at Sequoia and Kings Canyon National Parks. In our efforts to understand how wilderness management has evolved over time, including where and when particular actions have been taken, it became clear that the administrative history of wilderness management in Sequoia and Kings Canyon is poorly documented. Written documents are scattered about and much experiential knowledge exists only in people's heads and will shortly be entirely lost. This would be highly unfortunate because future wilderness management will not benefit from much that has already been learned. In addition, the parks are among the few true pioneers of wilderness management. This legacy of leadership and innovation should be celebrated. Much could be shared with the national and international wilderness management communities with just a modest investment in capturing and organizing experiential knowledge and administrative history. Advances in GIS technology allow much of this to be made spatially explicit. Much information could be organized by subzone (e.g. conditions, photographs, observations, management actions taken, trail reroutes)

The wilderness program would do well to follow the lead of the stock use and meadow management program in documenting historic use and conditions (Neuman 1990) and in making information spatially explicit.

Conclusion

The reinventory, in 2006-2007, of campsites first surveyed in the 1970s found that campsite conditions in the wilderness have improved greatly in the past 30 years. Current impacts are probably no more than one-third what they were in the 1970s. This improvement has occurred throughout the wilderness and is primarily the result of programs put in place by wilderness managers and implemented through the significant and ongoing efforts of field-located wilderness rangers. By concentrating use, maintaining established sites, eliminating new sites and impacts and educating users, they have succeeded in substantially improving the wilderness character of the Sequoia and Kings Canyon Wilderness.

Literature Cited

Cole, D. N. 1989. Wilderness campsite monitoring methods: a sourcebook. General Technical Report INT-259. USDA Forest Service, Intermountain Research Station, Ogden, Utah.

Cole, D. N. 1993. Campsites in three western wildernesses: Proliferation and changes in condition over 12 to 16 years. Research Paper INT-462. USDA Forest Service, Intermountain Research Station, Ogden, Utah.

Cole, D. N. and T. E. Ferguson. 2009. A relatively nonrestrictive approach to reducing campsite impact: Caney Creek Wilderness, Arkansas. *International Journal of Wilderness* 15: 20-25.

Cole, D. N., P. Foti and M. Brown. 2008. Twenty years of change on campsites in the backcountry of Grand Canyon National Park. *Environmental Management* 41: 959-970.

Farrell, T. A. and J. L. Marion. 1998. An evaluation of camping impacts and their management at Isle Royale National Park. USDI National Park Service Unpublished report, Isle Royale National Park, Houghton, Michigan.

Hall, T. E. 2001. Changes in wilderness campsite conditions resulting from implementation of a designated-site camping policy. USDA Forest Service Unpublished Report, Aldo Leopold Wilderness Research Institute, Missoula, Montana.

Hammitt, W. E. and D. N. Cole. 1998. Wildland recreation: Ecology and management, 2nd ed. John Wiley & Sons, New York, New York.

Leave No Trace. n.d. Leave No Trace--Outdoor ethics & skills: North America edition. Available from http://lnt.org/sites/default/files/NA.pdf (accessed 9 November 2012).

Marion, J. L. 1995. Capabilities and management utility of recreation impact monitoring programs. *Environmental Management* 19: 763-771.

McClaran, M. P. 1989. Recreational pack stock management in Sequoia and Kings Canyon National Parks. *Rangelands* 11(1): 3-8.

Neuman, Michael J. 1990. Past and present conditions of backcountry meadows in Sequoia and Kings Canyon National Parks. USDI National Park Service Unpublished Report, Sequoia and Kings Canyon National Parks, Three Rivers, California.

Parsons, D. J. 1979. The recovery of Bullfrog Lake. *Fremontia* 7(2): 9-13.

Parsons, D. J. 1983. Wilderness protection: an example from the southern Sierra Nevada, USA. *Environmental Conservation* 19: 23-30.

Parsons, D.J. 1986. Campsite impact data as a basis for determining wilderness use capacities. In: Lucas, Robert D., compiler. Proceedings National Wilderness Research Conference: Current Research; 1985 July 23-26; Fort Collins, Colorado. Gen. Tech. Rep. INT-212. Ogden, Utah: USDA Forest Service, Intermountain Research Station: 449-455.

Parsons, D. J. and S. A. MacLeod. 1980. Measuring impacts of wilderness use. *Parks* 5(3): 8-12.

Parsons, D. J., T. J. Stohlgren and P. A. Fodor. 1981. Establishing backcountry use quotas: an example from Mineral King, California. *Environmental Management* 5: 335-340.

Parsons, D. J. and T. J. Stohlgren. 1987. Impacts of visitor use on backcountry campsites in Sequoia and Kings Canyon National Parks, California. Technical Report No. 25. Cooperative National Park Resources Studies Unit, University of California, Davis, California.

Reid, S. E. and J. L. Marion. 2004. Effectiveness of a confinement strategy for reducing campsite impacts in Shenandoah National Park. *Environmental Conservation* 31: 274-282.

Stohlgren, T. J. and D. J. Parsons. 1986. Vegetation and soil recovery in campsites closed to visitor use. *Environmental Management* 10: 375-380.

Williams, P. B. and J. L. Marion. 1995. Assessing campsite conditions for limits of acceptable change management in Shenandoah National Park. Technical Report NPS/MARSHEN/NRTR-95/071. USDI National Park Service, Mid-Atlantic Region, Philadelphia, Pennsylvania.

Appendix 1: Number and condition of campsites in 2006-2007

Zone	Sub Zone	Zone/Subzone	Class 1 Camps	Class 2 Camps	Class 3 Camps	Class 4 Camps	Total Camp Sites	Humanly Restored Sites	Naturally Restored Sites	Total Restore Sites	Total Impacted Sites
28		**Goddard Canyon**									
28	01	Piute Creek Bridge	10	5	4	0	19	3	0	3	22
28	02	San Joaquin River	6	4	2	1	13	5	4	9	22
28	07	Martha Lake	3	3	0	0	6	1	10	11	17
33		**McClure**									
33	01	Lake 11110	7	0	0	0	7	2	6	8	15
33	02	Darwin Canyon	36	4	1	0	41	7	1	8	49
33	03	Evolution Meadow	29	14	1	0	44	9	12	21	65
33	04	McClure Meadow	13	9	2	2	26	17	9	26	52
33	05	Colby Meadow	26	14	2	1	43	19	24	43	86
33	06	South High Lakes	0	0	0	0	0	0	0	0	0
34		**Evolution**									
34	01	Evolution Lake	12	23	6	0	41	0	0	0	41
34	02	McGee Lakes	7	6	1	0	14	0	0	0	14
38		**Ionian Basin**									
38	02	Upper Blue Canyon	7	5	1	0	13	7	5	12	25
38	03	Lower Blue Canyon	5	0	1		6	1	4	5	11
39		**LeConte Canyon**									
39	01	Upper LeConte	20	10	3	0	33	2	4	6	39
39	02	Big Pete Meadow	11	10	3	0	24	4	2	6	30
39	03	Little Pete Meadow	5	3	1	0	9	3	1	4	13
39	04	LeConte R.S.	6	2	2	1	11	2	0	2	13
39	05	Ladder/Rambaud	13	0	0	0	13	6	1	7	20
39	06	Grouse Meadow	6	3	0	0	9	4	0	4	13
39	07	JMT - Simpson Junction	5	3	2	0	10	3	0	3	13
39	08	Deer Meadow	11	7	2	1	21	4	3	7	28
45		**Palisade Basin**									
45	01	Barrett Lakes	27	7	0	0	34	11	9	20	54
46		**Upper Basin**									
46	02	JMT - S. Fork Kings	25	10	2	0	37	12	7	19	56
46	04	Taboose Pass	11	5	0	0	16	1	4	5	21
46	06	Bench Lake	19	7	1	1	28	12	5	17	45
46	07	Lake Marjorie	28	8	0	0	36	7	3	10	46
47		**Cartridge Creek**									
47	01	Amphitheater Lake	9	3	0	0	12	6	4	10	22
47	04	Kid Lakes	11	3	0	0	14	1	10	11	25
51		**Tehipite-Simpson**									
51	04	Tehipite Valley	5	4	1	0	10	0	0	0	10
52		**Kennedy Pass**									
52	01	Kennedy Pass	32	5	0	0	37	8	4	12	49
53		**State Lakes**									
53	04	East Glacier Lakes	11	2	0	0	13	3	4	7	20

Zone	Sub Zone	Zone/Subzone	Class 1 Camps	Class 2 Camps	Class 3 Camps	Class 4 Camps	Total Camp Sites	Humanly Restored Sites	Naturally Restored Sites	Total Restore Sites	Total Impacted Sites
54		Granite Basin									
54	01	Granite Lake	12	4	1	1	0	17	0	0	17
54	02	Granite Basin Trail	18	2	0	0	20	4	3	7	27
54	05	South Granite Basin	4	0	0	0	4	0	0	0	4
54	07	Lower Tent Meadow	3	3	1	0	7	0	0	0	7
55		**Paradise Valley**									
55	01	Above Paradise Valley	8	6	2	0	16	3	6	9	25
58		**Woods Creek Junction**									
58	02	Castle Domes Meadow	4	2	2	0	8	2	2	4	12
61		**Sixty Lakes**									
61	01	Lower 60 Lakes	28	5	0	0	33	0	23	23	56
61	03	Upper 60 Lakes	5	2	0	0	7	0	2	2	9
62		**Rae Lakes**									
62	01	Dollar Lake	1	4	0	0	5	0	0	0	5
62	02	Arrowhead Lake	10	0	2	0	12	7	9	16	28
62	03	Rae Lakes 3	23	3	0	0	26	26	0	26	52
62	04	North Rae Lake 2	8	1	0	0	9	7	2	9	18
62	05	60 Lakes Pass Lake	1	0	0	0	1	2	1	3	4
62	06	South Rae Lake 2	28	12	4	0	44	25	5	30	74
62	07	Dragon Lake	3	2	0	0	5	0	0	0	5
63		**Charlotte Lake**									
63	01	Charlotte/Gardiner Trail	0	0	0	0	0	0	0	0	0
63	2	Below Charlotte Lake	1	1	1	0	3	1	3	4	7
63	03	Charlotte Lake	9	13	3	0	25	10	13	23	48
63	04	Vidette to Bullfrog	5	3	0	0	8	2	2	4	12
64		**Kearsarge Lakes**									
64	01	High Trail	3	1	0	0	4	3	3	6	10
64	02	Stream to Bullfrog	15	8	0	0	23	43	9	52	75
64	03	Lower Kearsarge Lake	10	2	1	0	13	0	6	6	19
64	04	Kearsarge Lakes 1 and 2	23	9	5	0	37	12	0	12	49
64	05	Kearsarge Lake 3	19	10	1	0	30	7	1	8	38
64	06	Upper Kearsarge Lake	9	1	0	0	10	0	0	0	10
65		**Center Basin/Vidette**									
65	03	JMT – Below Center B	24	11	7	3	45	17	27	44	89
65	04	Center Basin	13	3	3	0	19	3	13	16	35
65	05	JMT - N of Forester	15	10	1	0	26	3	5	8	34
66		**Bubbs Creek**									
66	02	Sphinx Creek	4	4	4	1	13	2	1	3	16
70		**Cloud Canyon**									
70	01	Big Brewer Lake	8	4	1	0	13	5	7	12	25
70	03	Cement Table	2	2	1	0	5	2	4	6	11
70	08	Colby Lake	7	2	2	0	11	1	6	7	18

Zone	Sub Zone	Zone/Subzone	Class 1 Camps	Class 2 Camps	Class 3 Camps	Class 4 Camps	Total Camp Sites	Humanly Restored Sites	Naturally Restored Sites	Total Restore Sites	Total Impacted Sites
72		**Sugarloaf Valley**									
72	01	Sugarloaf Valley	1	1	0	2	4	0	7	7	11
72	07	West Fork Ferguson Creek	3	1	0	0	4	0	1	1	5
73		**Seville Lake**									
73	04	Ranger Lake	4	8	1	0	13	3	0	3	16
74		**Mt. Silliman**									
74	03	Cahoon Gap	3	1	1	0	5	5	1	6	11
74	04	Silliman Lake	8	2	0	0	10	3	1	4	14
75		**Moose Lake**									
75	01	Table Meadow	9	0	0	0	9	2	3	5	14
75	03	Moose Lake	21	5	0	0	26	6	19	25	51
75	04	Tamarack Lake	14	6	1	1	22	10	4	14	36
77		**Middle Fork Kaweah**									
77	01	Panther Gap - Alta	5	8	4	0	17	4	0	4	21
77	02	Alta Meadow	4	2	0	0	6	2	4	6	12
79		**Kern-Kaweah**									
79	01	Milestone Creek	10	2	0	0	12	1	15	16	28
79	02	Upper Kern	4	0	0	0	4	2	19	21	25
79	03	Milestone Bowl	4	0	0	0	4	0	6	6	10
79	04	Upper Kern Kaweah	1	1	0	0	2	0	19	19	21
79	06	Lower Kern-Kaweah	2	1	0	0	3	0	10	10	13
79	07	Nine Lakes Basin	8	2	1	0	11	3	7	10	21
80		**Tyndall Creek**									
80	01	Lakes S of Forester	5	7	1	0	13	0	15	15	28
80	03	Shepherd Pass Lake	7	4	2	0	13	0	2	2	15
80	04	Below Lake South America	5	8	0	0	13	12	12	24	37
80	07	Lakes above Tyndall	3	6	1	1	11	8	1	9	20
80	08	Bighorn Plateau	4	0	0	0	4	2	0	2	6
81		**Wallace Creek**									
81	01	Wright Lakes	6	12	1	0	19	9	5	14	33
81	04	Upper Wallace Creek	4	14	1	0	19	20	16	36	55
83		**Crabtree**									
83	01	Guitar Lake	25	43	9	0	77	1	2	3	80
83	02	Sandy Meadow	4	3	0	0	7	7	1	8	15
83	03	Timberline to Guitar	5	2	0	0	7	2	0	2	9
83	04	Upper Whitney Creek	6	2	0	0	8	11	6	17	25
83	05	Crabtree R.S.	6	5	3	0	14	6	0	6	20
83	06	Timberline Lake	0	0	0	0	0	4	2	6	6
83	07	Hitchcock Lakes	6	1	0	0	7	6	4	10	17
83	08	Upper Crabtree Meadow	3	2	1	0	6	6	1	7	13
83	09	Lower Crabtree Meadow	10	4	0	1	15	12	4	16	31
83	10	Crabtree Lakes	8	5	0	0	13	6	3	9	22

Zone	Sub Zone	Zone/Subzone	Class 1 Camps	Class 2 Camps	Class 3 Camps	Class 4 Camps	Total Camp Sites	Humanly Restored Sites	Naturally Restored Sites	Total Restore Sites	Total Impacted Sites
84		**Rock Creek**									
84	01	Guyot Creek	4	1	0	0	5	0	0	0	5
84	02	Lower Rock Creek	13	4	5	2	24	15	3	18	42
84	03	Siberian Pass Trail	12	1	0	0	13	7	1	8	21
84	04	Funston - Forgotten	3	0	0	0	3	6	0	6	9
85		**Army Pass**									
85	01	Miter Basin - Sky Blue	5	3	0	0	8	2	0	2	10
85	02	Upper Rock Creek	11	5	0	0	16	3	2	5	21
85	03	Soldier Lake	17	9	4	0	30	21	3	24	54
85	04	Middle Rock Creek	11	4	2	1	18	20	6	26	44
86		**Funston Meadow**									
86	01	Kern Hot Springs	5	10	3	1	19	1	1	2	21
86	02	Upper Funston	4	2	1	2	9	1	3	4	13
86	03	Rattlesnake Crossing	6	2	2	0	10	3	0	3	13
86	04	Funston Meadow	3	1	0	1	5	3	0	3	8
86	05	Kern R.S.	4	4	0	0	8	0	8	8	16
87		**Chagoopa Plateau**									
87	01	Upper Big Arroyo	4	8	3	1	16	8	5	13	29
87	02	Low - Mid Big Arroyo	6	6	1	1	14	4	4	8	22
88		**Big Five Lakes**									
88	01	Long Lake	2	1	1	0	4	0	2	2	6
88	02	Lower Little Five	5	1	1	0	7	0	4	4	11
88	03	Mid - Upper Little Five	9	8	1	2	20	8	8	16	36
89		**Rattlesnake Creek**									
89	07	Little Claire Lake	6	2	0	0	8	0	3	3	11
90		**Hockett Meadow**									
90	01	Atwell - Hockett Trail	1	4	0	0	5	4	5	9	14
90	03	Horse Creek Crossing	3	3	2	0	8	1	2	3	11
90	06	Hockett Meadow	1	2	1	1	5	8	5	13	18
90	09	Sand Meadow	0	0	0	0	0	1	0	1	1
90	14	Quinn R.S. - Soda Creek	2	1	0	0	3	0	0	0	3
Total of All Subzones			1084	549	134	28	1795	616	544	1160	2955

Appendix 2: Summary campsite impact statistics for each subzone, 2006-2007

Zone	Sub Zone	Zone/Subzone	Mean Condition Class	Weighted Value	Weighted Value per Campable Mile	Weighted Value per Hectare
28		**Goddard Canyon**				
28	01	Piute Creek Bridge	1.68	166	277	302
28	02	San Joaquin River	1.85	183	87	13
28	07	Martha Lake	1.50	43	54	5
33		**McClure**				
33	01	Lake 11110	1.00	23	33	1
33	02	Darwin Canyon	1.15	106	76	8
33	03	Evolution Meadow	1.36	185	58	28
33	04	McClure Meadow	1.73	329	183	112
33	05	Colby Meadow	1.49	331	79	52
33	06	South High Lakes	0.00	0	0	0.0
34		**Evolution**				
34	01	Evolution Lake	1.85	330	138	51
34	02	McGee Lakes	1.57	73	28	6
38		**Ionian Basin**				
38	02	Upper Blue Canyon	1.54	91	61	3
38	03	Lower Blue Canyon	1.33	45	225	2
39		**LeConte Canyon**				
39	01	Upper LeConte	1.48	182	152	11
39	02	Big Pete Meadow	1.67	173	433	9
39	03	Little Pete Meadow	1.56	61	203	16
39	04	LeConte R.S.	1.82	157	785	34
39	05	Ladder/Rambaud	1.00	27	68	2
39	06	Grouse Meadow	1.33	32	107	4
39	07	JMT - Simpson Junction	1.70	89	445	8
39	08	Deer Meadow	1.67	202	253	19
45		**Palisade Basin**				
45	01	Barrett Lakes	1.21	109	68	6
46		**Upper Basin**				
46	02	JMT - S. Fork Kings	1.38	183	51	21
46	04	Taboose Pass	1.31	51	51	5
46	06	Bench Lake	1.43	200	286	19
46	07	Lake Marjorie	1.22	96	48	8
47		**Cartridge Creek**				
47	01	Amphitheater Lake	1.25	47	235	2
47	04	Kid Lakes	1.21	51	51	1
51		**Tehipite-Simpson**				
51	04	Tehipite Valley	1.60	59	98	2
52		**Kennedy Pass**				
52	01	Kennedy Pass	1.14	86	20	6
53		**State Lakes**				
53	04	East Glacier Lakes	1.15	37	62	6

Zone	Sub Zone	Zone/Subzone	Mean Condition Class	Weighted Value	Weighted Value per Campable Mile	Weighted Value per Hectare
54		**Granite Basin**				
54	01	Granite Lake	1.35	66	47	23
54	02	Granite Basin Trail	1.10	44	34	10
54	05	South Granite Basin	1.00	4	7	1
54	07	Lower Tent Meadow	1.71	51	128	5
55		**Paradise Valley**				
55	01	Above Paradise Valley	1.63	122	72	14
58		**Woods Creek Junction**				
58	02	Castle Domes Meadow	1.75	84	105	43
61		**Sixty Lakes**				
61	01	Lower 60 Lakes	1.15	104	29	9
61	03	Upper 60 Lakes	1.29	21	13	12
62		**Rae Lakes**				
62	01	Dollar Lake	1.80	25	50	12
62	02	Arrowhead Lake	1.33	102	85	39
62	03	Rae Lakes 3	1.12	93	78	63
62	04	North Rae Lake 2	1.11	32	36	20
62	05	60 Lakes Pass Lake	1.00	7	70	12
62	06	South Rae Lake 2	1.45	280	147	64
62	07	Dragon Lake	1.40	15	50	3
63		**Charlotte Lake**				
63	01	Charlotte/Gardiner Trail	0.00	0	0	0
63	2	Below Charlotte Lake	2.00	45	225	24
63	03	Charlotte Lake	1.76	223	186	32
63	04	Vidette to Bullfrog	1.38	31	310	51
64		**Kearsarge Lakes**				
64	01	High Trail	1.25	21	105	6
64	02	Stream to Bullfrog	1.35	167	128	217
64	03	Lower Kearsarge Lake	1.31	64	460	221
64	04	Kearsarge Lakes 1 and 2	1.51	251	314	292
64	05	Kearsarge Lake 3	1.40	125	156	176
64	06	Upper Kearsarge Lake	1.10	15	75	9
65		**Center Basin/Vidette**				
65	03	JMT – Below Center Basin	1.76	613	557	72
65	04	Center Basin	1.47	153	153	15
65	05	JMT – N of Forester	1.46	121	151	11
66		**Bubbs Creek**				
66	02	Sphinx Creek	2.15	229	153	32
70		**Cloud Canyon**				
70	01	Big Brewer Lake	1.46	86	45	7
70	03	Cement Table	1.80	56	47	16
70	08	Colby Lake	1.55	93	47	7

Zone	Sub Zone	Zone/Subzone	Mean Condition Class	Weighted Value	Weighted Value per Campable Mile	Weighted Value per Hectare
72		**Sugarloaf Valley**				
72	01	Sugarloaf Valley	2.75	171	49	19
72	07	West Fork Ferguson Creek	1.25	11	2	1
73		**Seville Lake**				
73	04	Ranger Lake	1.77	88	147	27
74		**Mt. Silliman**				
74	03	Cahoon Gap	1.60	51	26	24
74	04	Silliman Lake	1.20	28	35	2
75		**Moose Lake**				
75	01	Table Meadow	1.00	19	16	4
75	03	Moose Lake	1.19	101	144	10
75	04	Tamarack Lake	1.50	183	153	9
77		**Middle Fork Kaweah**				
77	01	Panther Gap - Alta	1.94	181	453	21
77	02	Alta Meadow	1.33	28	47	6
79		**Kern-Kaweah**				
79	01	Milestone Creek	1.17	54	90	2
79	02	Upper Kern	1.00	46	115	13
79	03	Milestone Bowl	1.00	16	8	2
79	04	Upper Kern Kaweah	1.50	45	14	3
79	06	Lower Kern-Kaweah	1.33	28	93	2
79	07	Nine Lakes Basin	1.36	70	350	8
80		**Tyndall Creek**				
80	01	Lakes S of Forester	1.69	107	535	10
80	03	Shepherd Pass Lake	1.62	95	950	41
80	04	Below Lake South America	1.62	101	112	7
80	07	Lakes above Tyndall	2.00	162	810	83
80	08	Bighorn Plateau	1.00	8	40	1
81		**Wallace Creek**				
81	01	Wright Lakes	1.74	136	170	7
81	04	Upper Wallace Creek	1.84	190	106	18
83		**Crabtree**				
83	01	Guitar Lake	1.79	559	1398	87
83	02	Sandy Meadow	1.43	38	19	4
83	03	Timberline to Guitar	1.29	21	70	11
83	04	Upper Whitney Creek	1.25	52	40	25
83	05	Crabtree R.S.	1.79	138	92	131
83	06	Timberline Lake	0.00	12	120	16
83	07	Hitchcock Lakes	1.14	32	53	11
83	08	Upper Crabtree Meadow	1.67	59	33	42
83	09	Lower Crabtree Meadow	1.47	141	94	6
83	10	Crabtree Lakes	1.38	56	18	5

Zone	Sub Zone	Zone/Subzone	Mean Condition Class	Weighted Value	Weighted Value per Campable Mile	Weighted Value per Hectare
84		**Rock Creek**				
84	01	Guyot Creek	1.20	10	100	1
84	02	Lower Rock Creek	1.83	373	124	18
84	03	Siberian Pass Trail	1.08	34	68	2
84	04	Funston - Forgotten	1.00	15	15	1
85		**Army Pass**				
85	01	Miter Basin - Sky Blue	1.38	27	54	4
85	02	Upper Rock Creek	1.31	51	51	3
85	03	Soldier Lake	1.57	239	184	20
85	04	Middle Rock Creek	1.61	222	106	51
86		**Funston Meadow**				
86	01	Kern Hot Springs	2.00	234	1170	144
86	02	Upper Funston	2.11	204	340	29
86	03	Rattlesnake Crossing	1.60	84	210	19
86	04	Funston Meadow	1.80	90	129	13
86	05	Kern R.S.	1.50	44	28	10
87		**Chagoopa Plateau**				
87	01	Upper Big Arroyo	2.06	243	61	16
87	02	Low - Mid Big Arroyo	1.79	163	30	6
88		**Big Five Lakes**				
88	01	Long Lake	1.75	42	53	9
88	02	Lower Little Five	1.43	49	123	55
88	03	Mid - Upper Little Five	1.80	269	192	50
89		**Rattlesnake Creek**				
89	07	Little Claire Lake	1.25	24	80	16
90		**Hockett Meadow**				
90	01	Atwell - Hockett Trail	1.80	43	430	2
90	03	Horse Creek Crossing	1.88	87	290	58
90	06	Hockett Meadow	2.40	144	480	16
90	09	Sand Meadow	0.00	2	3	1
90	14	Quinn R.S. - Soda Creek	1.33	8	40	1
Mean for All Subzones			1.50	144	123	14.5

Appendix 3: Campsite impact by subzone, ordered beginning with those with the lowest weighted value per campable mile

Zone	Subzone Number	Subzone Name	Weighted Value per Campable Mile, 2006-2007	Weighted Value, 2006-2007	Number of Campsites, 2006-2007	Number of Campsites per Campable Mile, 2006-2007	Number of Impacted Sites, 2006-2007	Number of Impacted Sites per Campable Mile, 2006-2007
33	06	South High Lakes	0	0	0	0.0	0	0.0
63	01	Charlotte/Gardiner Trail	0	0	0	0.0	0	0.0
90	09	Sand Meadow	2	1	0	0.0	1	1.7
72	07	West Fork Ferguson Creek	2	11	4	0.7	5	0.9
79	03	Milestone Bowl	5	10	4	2.0	10	5.0
54	05	South Granite Basin	7	4	4	6.7	4	6.7
84	04	Funston - Forgotten	9	9	3	3.0	9	9.0
75	01	Table Meadow	12	14	9	7.5	14	11.7
61	03	Upper 60 Lakes	14	22	7	4.4	9	5.6
52	01	Kennedy Pass	19	82	37	8.4	49	11.1
83	10	Crabtree Lakes	21	64	13	4.2	22	7.1
33	01	Lake 11110	21	15	7	10.0	15	21.4
79	04	Upper Kern-Kaweah	22	74	2	0.6	21	6.4
83	02	Sandy Meadow	24	47	7	3.5	15	7.5
61	01	Lower 60 Lakes	27	98	33	9.2	56	15.6
34	02	McGee Lakes	28	73	14	5.4	14	5.4
80	08	Bighorn Plateau	30	6	4	20.0	6	30.0
62	04	North Rae Lake 2	31	28	9	10.0	18	20.0
54	02	Granite Basin Trail	31	41	20	15.4	27	20.8
74	04	Silliman Lake	35	28	10	12.5	14	17.5
86	05	Kern Ranger Station	35	56	8	5.0	16	10.0
62	05	60 Lakes Pass Lake	40	4	1	10.0	4	40.0
90	14	Quinn Ranger Station - Soda Creek	40	8	3	15.0	3	15.0
87	02	Lower - Mid Big Arroyo	43	231	14	2.6	22	4.1
74	03	Cahoon Gap	43	86	5	2.5	11	5.5
83	04	Upper Whitney Creek	43	56	8	6.2	25	19.2
54	01	Granite Lake	47	66	17	12.1	17	12.1
46	07	Lake Marjorie	49	97	36	18.0	46	23.0
83	07	Hitchcock Lakes	49	29	7	11.7	17	28.3
39	05	Ladder/Rambaud	50	20	13	32.5	20	50.0
62	01	Dollar Lake	50	25	5	10.0	5	10.0
62	07	Dragon Lake	50	15	5	16.7	5	16.7
47	04	Kid Lakes	52	52	14	14.0	25	25.0
77	02	Alta Meadow	53	32	6	10.0	12	20.0
46	04	Taboose Pass	54	54	16	16.0	21	21.0
85	02	Upper Rock Creek	54	54	16	16.0	21	21.0

Zone	Subzone Number	Subzone Name	Weighted Value per Campable Mile, 2006-2007	Weighted Value, 2006-2007	Number of Campsites, 2006-2007	Number of Campsites per Campable Mile, 2006-2007	Number of Impacted Sites, 2006-2007	Number of Impacted Sites per Campable Mile, 2006-2007
83	08	Upper Crabtree Meadow	54	98	6	3.3	13	7.2
85	01	Miter Basin - Sky Blue	58	29	8	16.0	10	20.0
84	03	Siberian Pass Trail	58	29	13	26.0	21	42.0
53	04	East Glacier Lakes	59	35	13	21.7	20	33.3
83	06	Timberline Lake	60	6	0	0.0	6	60.0
46	02	JMT - S. Fork Kings	61	219	37	10.3	56	15.6
79	02	Upper Kern	63	25	4	10.0	25	62.5
70	01	Big Brewer Lake	63	119	13	6.8	25	13.2
70	08	Colby Lake	65	129	11	5.5	18	9.0
33	03	Evolution Meadow	66	211	44	13.8	65	20.3
62	03	Rae Lakes 3	68	82	26	21.7	52	43.3
45	01	Barrett Lakes	68	110	34	21.3	54	33.8
88	01	Long Lake	71	57	4	5.0	6	7.5
83	03	Timberline to Guitar	73	22	7	23.3	9	30.0
28	07	Martha Lake	74	60	6	7.5	17	21.3
64	06	Upper Kearsarge Lake	75	15	10	50.0	10	50.0
33	02	Darwin Canyon	77	108	41	29.3	49	35.0
70	03	Cement Table	81	97	5	4.2	11	9.2
89	07	Little Claire Lake	83	25	8	26.7	11	36.7
79	01	Milestone Creek	86	51	12	20.0	28	46.7
38	02	Upper Blue Canyon	86	129	13	8.7	25	16.7
55	01	Above Paradise Valley	96	163	16	9.4	25	14.7
87	01	Upper Big Arroyo	98	393	16	4.0	29	7.3
51	04	Tehipite Valley	98	59	10	16.7	10	16.7
84	01	Guyot Creek	100	10	5	50.0	5	50.0
64	01	High Trail	113	23	4	20.0	10	50.0
39	06	Grouse Meadow	116	35	9	30.0	13	43.3
79	06	Lower Kern-Kaweah	116	35	3	10.0	13	43.3
33	05	Colby Meadow	117	490	43	10.2	86	20.5
83	05	Crabtree Ranger Station	120	180	14	9.3	20	13.3
72	01	Sugarloaf Valley	123	432	4	1.1	11	3.1
54	07	Lower Tent Meadow	128	51	7	17.5	7	17.5
28	02	San Joaquin River	133	279	13	6.2	22	10.5
62	02	Arrowhead Lake	136	163	12	10.0	28	23.3
34	01	Evolution Lake	138	330	41	17.1	41	17.1
58	02	Castle Domes Meadow	143	114	8	10.0	12	15.0
75	03	Moose Lake	143	100	26	37.1	51	72.9

Zone	Subzone	Subzone Name	Weighted Value per Campable Mile, 2006-2007	Weighted Value, 2006-2007	Number of Campsites, 2006-2007	Number of Campsites per Campable Mile, 2006-2007	Number of Impacted Sites, 2006-2007	Number of Impacted Sites per Campable Mile, 2006-2007
83	09	Lower Crabtree Meadow	150	225	15	10.0	31	20.7
64	02	Stream to Bullfrog	158	205	23	17.7	75	57.7
88	02	Lower Little Five Lakes	161	64	7	17.5	11	27.5
39	01	Upper LeConte	167	201	33	27.5	39	32.5
80	04	Below Lake South America	168	151	13	14.4	37	41.1
73	04	Ranger Lake	168	101	13	21.7	16	26.7
65	05	JMT – N of Forester	172	137	26	32.5	34	42.5
64	05	Kearsarge Lake 3	173	138	30	37.5	38	47.5
66	02	Sphinx Creek	183	274	13	8.7	16	10.7
81	04	Upper Wallace Creek	190	342	19	10.6	55	30.6
64	03	Lower Kearsarge Lake	190	76	13	32.5	19	47.5
86	04	Funston Meadow	192	134	5	7.1	8	11.4
62	06	South Rae Lake 2	195	370	44	23.2	74	38.9
84	02	Lower Rock Creek	197	590	24	8.0	42	14.0
85	04	Middle Rock Creek	198	416	18	8.6	44	21.0
75	04	Tamarack Lake	211	254	22	18.3	36	30.0
65	04	Center Basin	223	223	19	19.0	35	35.0
81	01	Wright Lakes	234	188	19	23.8	33	41.3
47	01	Amphitheater Lake	248	50	12	60.0	22	110.0
86	03	Rattlesnake Crossing	254	101	10	25.0	13	32.5
39	03	Little Pete Meadow	255	77	9	30.0	13	43.3
85	03	Soldier Lake	264	344	30	23.1	54	41.5
63	03	Charlotte Lake	283	340	25	20.8	48	40.0
88	03	Mid - Upper Little Five Lakes	305	427	20	14.3	36	25.7
33	04	McClure Meadow	308	554	26	14.4	52	28.9
28	01	Piute Creek Bridge	309	185	19	31.7	22	36.7
39	08	Deer Meadow	313	251	21	26.3	28	35.0
38	03	Lower Blue Canyon	321	64	6	30.0	11	55.0
63	04	Vidette to Bullfrog	345	35	8	80.0	12	120.0
90	03	Horse Creek Crossing	371	111	8	26.7	11	36.7
64	04	Kearsarge Lakes 1 and 2	376	301	37	46.3	49	61.3
46	06	Bench Lake	381	267	28	40.0	45	64.3
63	2	Below Charlotte Lake	432	86	3	15.0	7	35.0
86	02	Upper Funston	472	283	9	15.0	13	21.7
79	07	Nine Lakes Basin	477	95	11	55.0	21	105.0
39	02	Big Pete Meadow	503	201	24	60.0	30	75.0

Zone	Subzone Number	Subzone Name	Weighted Value per Campable Mile, 2006-2007	Weighted Value, 2006-2007	Number of Campsites, 2006-2007	Number of Campsites per Campable Mile, 2006-2007	Number of Impacted Sites, 2006-2007	Number of Impacted Sites per Campable Mile, 2006-2007
77	01	Panther Gap - Alta	534	214	17	42.5	21	52.5
39	07	JMT - Simpson Junction	540	108	10	50.0	13	65.0
90	01	Atwell - Hockett Trail	700	70	5	50.0	14	140.0
80	01	JMT N of Forester Pass	829	166	13	65.0	28	140.0
39	04	LeConte Ranger Station	904	181	11	55.0	13	65.0
65	03	JMT – below Center Basin	944	1038	45	40.9	89	80.9
80	03	Shepherd Pass Lake	1050	105	13	130.0	15	150.0
86	01	Kern Hot Springs	1271	254	19	95.0	21	105.0
80	07	Lakes above Tyndall	1309	262	11	55.0	20	100.0
90	06	Hockett Meadow	1416	425	5	16.7	18	60.0
83	01	Guitar Lake	1436	575	77	192.5	80	200.0

Appendix 4: Number of campsites at various distances from water, 2006-2007

Zone	Sub Zone	Zone/Subzone	More Than 100 Feet From Water	50 to 100 Feet From Water	25 to 50 Feet From Water	Less Than 25 Feet From Water
28		Goddard Canyon				
28	01	Piute Creek Bridge	11	2	3	3
28	02	San Joaquin River	5	2	2	4
28	07	Martha Lake	0	0	4	2
33		McClure				
33	01	Lake 11110	2	4	0	1
33	02	Darwin Canyon	24	7	8	2
33	03	Evolution Meadow	26	5	10	3
33	04	McClure Meadow	11	3	7	5
33	05	Colby Meadow	17	18	8	0
33	06	South High Lakes	0	0	0	0
34		Evolution				
34	01	Evolution Lake	22	6	6	7
34	02	McGee Lakes	4	4	4	2
38		Ionian Basin				
38	02	Upper Blue Canyon	13	0	0	0
38	03	Lower Blue Canyon	2	2	1	1
39		LeConte Canyon				
39	01	Upper LeConte	22	8	2	1
39	02	Big Pete Meadow	14	7	1	2
39	03	Little Pete Meadow	8	0	1	2
39	04	LeConte R.S.	5	5	1	0
39	05	Ladder/Rambaud	10	2	1	0
39	06	Grouse Meadow	5	2	2	0
39	07	JMT - Simpson Junction	7	1	2	0
39	08	Deer Meadow	13	6	2	0
45		Palisade Basin				
45	01	Barrett Lakes	29	4	1	0
46		Upper Basin				
46	02	JMT - S. Fork Kings	13	19	5	0
46	04	Taboose Pass	9	6	1	0
46	06	Bench Lake	15	3	3	7
46	07	Lake Marjorie	29	3	2	2
47		Cartridge Creek				
47	01	Amphitheater Lake	10	2	0	0
47	04	Kid Lakes	1	5	5	3
51		Tehipite-Simpson				
51	04	Tehipite Valley	5	4	1	0
52		Kennedy Pass				
52	01	Kennedy Pass	23	10	4	0
53		State Lakes				
53	04	East Glacier Lakes	6	3	2	2

Zone	Sub Zone	Zone/Subzone	More Than 100 Feet From Water	50 to 100 Feet From Water	25 to 50 Feet From Water	Less Than 25 Feet From Water
54		**Granite Basin**				
54	01	Granite Lake	13	3	1	0
54	02	Granite Basin Trail	11	4	3	2
54	05	South Granite Basin	4	0	0	0
54	07	Lower Tent Meadow	3	4	0	0
55		**Paradise Valley**				
55	01	Above Paradise Valley	15	1	0	0
58		**Woods Creek Junction**				
58	02	Castle Domes Meadow	6	0	1	1
61		**Sixty Lakes**				
61	01	Lower 60 Lakes	5	12	13	3
61	03	Upper 60 Lakes	1	5	1	0
62		**Rae Lakes**				
62	01	Dollar Lake	2	0	3	0
62	02	Arrowhead Lake	9	0	1	2
62	03	Rae Lakes 3	19	3	3	1
62	04	North Rae Lake 2	6	3	0	0
62	05	60 Lakes Pass Lake	1	0	0	0
62	06	South Rae Lake 2	39	4	0	1
62	07	Dragon Lake	3	0	0	2
63		**Charlotte Lake**				
63	01	Charlotte/Gardiner Trail	0	0	0	0
63	2	Below Charlotte Lk	0	1	2	0
63	03	Charlotte Lake	20	5	0	0
63	04	Vidette to Bullfrog	2	3	3	0
64		**Kearsarge Lakes**				
64	01	High Trail	4	0	0	0
64	02	Stream to Bullfrog	18	4	1	0
64	03	Lower Kearsarge Lake	6	3	3	1
64	04	Kearsarge Lakes 1 and 2	30	3	3	1
64	05	Kearsarge Lake 3	17	7	2	4
64	06	Upper Kearsarge Lk	6	1	2	1
65		**Center Basin/Vidette**				
65	03	JMT – Below Center	25	13	4	3
65	04	Center Basin	10	5	4	0
65	05	JMT - N of Forester	14	10	2	0
66		**Bubbs Creek**				
66	02	Sphinx Creek	8	1	3	1
70		**Cloud Canyon**				
70	01	Big Brewer Lake	8	1	3	1
70	03	Cement Table	3	2	0	0
70	08	Colby Lake	2	6	1	2

Zone	Subzone	Zone/Subzone	More Than 100 Feet From Water	50 to 100 Feet From Water	25 to 50 Feet From Water	Less Than 25 Feet From Water
72		**Sugarloaf Valley**				
72	01	Sugarloaf Valley	3	1	0	0
72	07	West Fork Ferguson Creek	1	3	0	0
73		**Seville Lake**				
73	04	Ranger Lake	10	3	0	0
74		**Mt. Silliman**				
74	03	Cahoon Gap	5	0	0	0
74	04	Silliman Lake	6	1	2	1
75		**Moose Lake**				
75	01	Table Meadow	2	2	2	3
75	03	Moose Lake	16	4	4	2
75	04	Tamarack Lake	16	4	1	1
77		**Middle Fork Kaweah**				
77	01	Panther Gap - Alta	9	4	3	1
77	02	Alta Meadow	3	1	2	0
79		**Kern-Kaweah**				
79	01	Milestone Creek	5	5	1	1
79	02	Upper Kern	1	1	2	0
79	03	Milestone Bowl	1	3	0	0
79	04	Upper Kern Kaweah	0	1	1	0
79	06	Lower Kern-Kaweah	1	1	1	0
79	07	Nine Lakes Basin	9	1	0	1
80		**Tyndall Creek**				
80	01	Lakes S of Forester Pass	2	7	1	3
80	03	Shepherd Pass Lake	8	2	2	1
80	04	Below Lake South America	4	8	1	0
80	07	Lakes above Tyndall	9	1	1	0
80	08	Bighorn Plateau	2	1	1	0
81		**Wallace Creek**				
81	01	Wright Lakes	16	1	1	1
81	04	Upper Wallace Creek	8	5	5	1
83		**Crabtree**				
83	01	Guitar Lake	56	10	4	7
83	02	Sandy Meadow	3	1	3	0
83	03	Timberline to Guitar	1	2	3	1
83	04	Upper Whitney Creek	4	2	2	0
83	05	Crabtree R.S.	13	0	1	0
83	06	Timberline Lake	0	0	0	0
83	07	Hitchcock Lakes	0	2	2	3
83	08	Upper Crabtree Meadow	5	0	1	0
83	09	Lower Crabtree Meadow	11	4	0	0
83	10	Crabtree Lakes	6	4	2	1

Zone	Subzone	Zone/Subzone	More Than 100 Feet From Water	50 to 100 Feet From Water	25 to 50 Feet From Water	Less Than 25 Feet From Water
84		Rock Creek				
84	01	Guyot Creek	3	0	2	0
84	02	Lower Rock Creek	12	10	1	1
84	03	Siberian Pass Trail	12	1	0	0
84	04	Funston - Forgotten	2	0	1	0
85		Army Pass				
85	01	Miter Basin - Sky Blue	4	2	2	0
85	02	Upper Rock Creek	8	1	4	3
85	03	Soldier Lake	23	5	2	0
85	04	Middle Rock Creek	13	3	2	0
86		Funston Meadow				
86	01	Kern Hot Springs	7	8	2	2
86	02	Upper Funston	3	3	1	2
86	03	Rattlesnake Crossing	6	3	1	0
86	04	Funston Meadow	2	0	1	2
86	05	Kern R.S.	3	5	0	0
87		Chagoopa Plateau				
87	01	Upper Big Arroyo	9	6	1	0
87	02	Lower - Mid Big Arroyo	8	5	1	0
88		Big Five Lakes				
88	01	Long Lake	4	0	0	0
88	02	Lower Little Five	5	1	1	0
88	03	Mid - Upper Little Five	13	6	1	0
89		Rattlesnake Creek				
89	07	Little Claire Lake	7	1	0	0
90		Hockett Meadow				
90	01	Atwell - Hockett Trail	4	0	1	0
90	03	Horse Creek Crossing	3	4	0	1
90	06	Hockett Meadow	4	1	0	0
90	09	Sand Meadow	0	0	0	0
90	14	Quinn R.S. - Soda Creek	2	0	1	0

Appendix 5: Change in number and condition of campsites since the late 1970s

The following subzones contain areas within them that were surveyed in 2006-2007 but not in the late 1970s: 45-1 (Barrett Lakes), 46-6 (Bench Lake), 47-1 (Amphitheater Lake), 64-2 (Stream to Bullfrog), 75-3 (Moose Lake), 75-4 (Tamarack Lake), 80-3 (Shepherd Pass Lake), and 83-1 (Guitar Lake). As a result, estimates of change in these subzones are somewhat misleading. The improvement in conditions that occurred in all of these subzones other than 80-3 (Shepherd Pass Lake) is underestimated and the deterioration in conditions that occurred in the 80-3 (Shepherd Pass Lake) subzone is overestimated.

Zone	Sub Zone	Zone/Subzone	Campsites, 1976-81	Impacted Sites, 2006-7	Mean Condition Class, 1976-81	Mean Condition Class, 2006-7	Weighted Value, 1976-81	Weighted Value, 2006-7
28		Goddard Canyon						
28	01	Piute Creek Bridge	22	22	2.55	1.68	783	166
28	02	San Joaquin River	20	22	3.20	1.85	1155	183
28	07	Martha Lake	8	17	1.50	1.50	47	43
33		McClure						
33	01	Lake 11110	9	15	1.33	1.00	24	23
33	02	Darwin Canyon	79	49	1.91	1.15	1131	106
33	03	Evolution Meadow	68	65	2.31	1.36	1818	185
33	04	McClure Meadow	24	52	3.21	1.73	1485	329
33	05	Colby Meadow	83	86	2.39	1.49	2204	331
33	06	South High Lakes	3	0	2.33	0.00	42	0
34		Evolution						
34	01	Evolution Lake	57	41	2.18	1.85	1000	330
34	02	McGee Lakes	80	14	2.03	1.57	1165	73
38		Ionian Basin						
38	02	Upper Blue Canyon	23	25	2.39	1.54	665	91
38	03	Lower Blue Canyon	13	11	2.08	1.33	269	45
39		LeConte Canyon						
39	01	Upper LeConte	35	39	2.06	1.48	659	91
39	02	Big Pete Meadow	42	30	2.07	1.67	666	173
39	03	Little Pete Meadow	13	13	2.92	1.56	539	61
39	04	LeConte R.S.	29	13	2.45	1.82	876	157
39	05	Ladder/Rambaud	18	20	1.67	1.00	78	27
39	06	Grouse Meadow	19	13	2.79	1.33	810	32
39	07	JMT - Simpson Junction	13	13	3.08	1.70	710	89
39	08	Deer Meadow	19	28	3.37	1.67	1199	202
45		Palisade Basin						
45	01	Barrett Lakes*	59	54	1.37	1.21	207	109
46		Upper Basin						
46	02	JMT - S. Fork Kings	69	56	1.83	1.38	850	183
46	04	Taboose Pass	17	21	2.24	1.31	276	51
46	06	Bench Lake*	41	45	2.37	1.43	1079	200
46	07	Lake Marjorie	66	46	1.62	1.22	600	96
47		Cartridge Creek						
47	01	Amphitheater Lake*	14	22	1.36	1.25	58	47
47	04	Kid Lakes	29	25	1.31	1.21	93	51
51		Tehipite-Simpson						
51	04	Tehipite Valley	27	10	1.89	1.60	481	59
52		Kennedy Pass						
52	01	Kennedy Pass	58	49	1.67	1.14	405	86
53		State Lakes						
53	04	East Glacier Lakes	22	20	1.68	1.15	135	37

Zone	Sub Zone	Zone/Subzone	Campsites, 1976-81	Impacted Sites, 2006-7	Mean Condition Class, 1976-81	Mean Condition Class, 2006-7	Weighted Value, 1976-81	Weighted Value, 2006-7
54		Granite Basin						
54	01	Granite Lake	51	17	2.08	1.35	757	66
54	02	Granite Basin Trail	42	27	2.02	1.10	616	44
54	05	South Granite Basin	17	4	1.41	1.00	109	4
54	07	Lower Tent Meadow	16	7	2.88	1.71	736	51
55		Paradise Valley						
55	01	Above Paradise Valley	34	25	2.15	1.63	626	122
58		Woods Creek Junction						
58	02	Castle Domes Meadow	23	12	2.70	1.75	703	84
61		Sixty Lakes						
61	01	Lower 60 Lakes	91	56	1.52	1.15	596	104
61	03	Upper 60 Lakes	17	9	2.88	1.29	707	21
62		Rae Lakes						
62	01	Dollar Lake	21	5	2.38	1.80	514	25
62	02	Arrowhead Lake	55	28	1.80	1.33	722	102
62	03	Rae Lakes 3	70	52	2.11	1.12	1295	93
62	04	North Rae Lake 2	36	18	1.83	1.11	300	32
62	05	60 Lakes Pass Lake	5	4	2.00	1.00	49	7
62	06	South Rae Lake 2	118	74	2.25	1.45	2688	280
62	07	Dragon Lake	18	5	1.78	1.40	185	15
63		Charlotte Lake						
63	01	Charlotte/Gardiner Trail	11	0	2.18	0.00	173	0
63	2	Below Charlotte Lk	4	7	3.25	2.00	216	45
63	03	Charlotte Lake	73	48	2.77	1.76	3103	223
63	04	Vidette to Bullfrog	10	12	2.50	1.25	237	21
64		Kearsarge Lakes						
64	01	High Trail	12	10	2.50	1.25	237	21
64	02	Stream to Bullfrog*	35	75	2.34	1.35	736	167
64	03	Lower Kearsarge Lk	40	19	2.23	1.31	939	64
64	04	Kearsarge Lakes 1 and 2	51	49	2.37	1.51	1497	251
64	05	Kearsarge Lake 3	44	38	2.50	1.40	1565	125
64	06	Upper Kearsarge Lk	15	10	1.53	1.10	93	15
65		Center Basin/Vidette						
65	03	JMT – Below Center	79	89	2.04	1.76	1583	613
65	04	Center Basin	32	35	1.84	1.47	420	153
65	05	JMT - N of Forester	33	34	2.03	1.46	564	121
66		Bubbs Creek						
66	02	Sphinx Creek	27	16	2.85	2.15	1221	229
70		Cloud Canyon						
70	01	Big Brewer Lake	31	25	1.65	1.46	325	86
70	03	Cement Table	12	11	2.42	1.80	522	56
70	08	Colby Lake	20	18	2.00	1.55	386	93

Zone	Sub Zone	Zone/Subzone	Campsites, 1976-81	Impacted Sites, 2006-7	Mean Condition Class, 1976-81	Mean Condition Class, 2006-7	Weighted Value, 1976-81	Weighted Value, 2006-7
72		**Sugarloaf Valley**						
72	01	Sugarloaf Valley	17	11	1.82	2.75	353	171
72	07	West Fork Ferguson Creek	11	5	1.91	1.25	139	11
73		**Seville Lake**						
73	04	Ranger Lake	41	16	2.12	1.77	885	88
74		**Mt. Silliman**						
74	03	Cahoon Gap	24	11	1.83	1.60	162	51
74	04	Silliman Lake	14	14	1.79	1.20	107	28
75		**Moose Lake**						
75	01	Table Meadow	11	14	1.64	1.00	84	19
75	03	Moose Lake*	53	51	1.25	1.19	137	101
75	04	Tamarack Lake*	28	36	2.68	1.50	1178	183
77		**Middle Fork Kaweah**						
77	01	Panther Gap - Alta	25	21	2.04	1.94	309	191
77	02	Alta Meadow	29	12	1.97	1.33	283	28
79		**Kern-Kaweah**						
79	01	Milestone Creek	21	28	1.67	1.17	188	54
79	02	Upper Kern	7	25	1.71	1.00	32	46
79	03	Milestone Bowl	13	10	1.31	1.00	33	16
79	04	Upper Kern-Kaweah	26	21	1.50	1.50	188	45
79	06	Lower Kern-Kaweah	19	13	1.95	1.33	166	28
79	07	Nine Lakes Basin	8	21	2.00	1.36	48	70
80		**Tyndall Creek**						
80	01	Lakes S of Forester	16	28	1.38	1.69	65	107
80	03	Shepherd Pass Lake*	6	15	1.50	1.62	21	95
80	04	Below Lake South America	41	37	1.88	1.62	396	101
80	07	Lakes above Tyndall	26	20	2.08	2.00	447	162
80	08	Bighorn Plateau	4	6	1.25	1.00	9	8
81		**Wallace Creek**						
81	01	Wright Lakes	36	33	1.69	1.74	372	136
81	04	Upper Wallace Creek	43	55	2.00	1.84	638	190
83		**Crabtree**						
83	01	Guitar Lake*	56	80	2.29	1.79	1123	559
83	02	Sandy Meadow	30	15	1.60	1.43	177	38
83	03	Timberline to Guitar	9	9	1.56	1.29	53	21
83	04	Upper Whitney Creek	39	25	2.23	1.25	809	52
83	05	Crabtree R.S.	28	20	3.07	1.79	1622	138
83	06	Timberline Lake	19	6	1.74	0.00	167	12
83	07	Hitchcock Lakes	17	17	1.12	1.14	27	32
83	08	Upper Crabtree Meadow	22	13	2.14	1.67	650	59
83	09	Lower Crabtree Meadow	30	31	2.13	1.47	751	141
83	10	Crabtree Lakes	27	22	2.15	1.38	575	56

Zone	Sub Zone	Zone/Subzone	Campsites, 1976-81	Impacted Sites, 2006-7	Mean Condition Class, 1976-81	Mean Condition Class, 2006-7	Weighted Value, 1976-81	Weighted Value, 2006-7
84		**Rock Creek**						
84	01	Guyot Creek	4	5	2.50	1.20	72	10
84	02	Lower Rock Creek	23	42	2.96	1.83	1146	373
84	03	Siberian Pass Trail	11	21	1.36	1.08	31	34
84	04	Funston - Forgotten	12	9	1.75	1.00	114	15
85		**Army Pass**						
85	01	Miter Basin - Sky Blue	18	10	1.44	1.38	96	27
85	02	Upper Rock Creek	17	21	2.18	1.31	311	51
85	03	Soldier Lake	52	54	2.48	1.57	1641	239
85	04	Middle Rock Creek	44	44	2.43	4.61	1330	222
86		**Funston Meadow**						
86	01	Kern Hot Springs	16	21	2.38	2.00	299	234
86	02	Upper Funston	10	13	2.90	2.11	449	204
86	03	Rattlesnake Crossing	15	13	2.13	1.60	216	84
86	04	Funston Meadow	10	8	2.10	1.80	103	90
86	05	Kern R.S.	14	16	2.43	1.50	378	44
87		**Chagoopa Plateau**						
87	01	Upper Big Arroyo	31	29	1.77	2.06	455	243
87	02	Lower - Mid Big Arroyo	45	22	1.76	1.79	576	163
88		**Big Five Lakes**						
88	01	Long Lake	14	6	2.36	1.75	354	42
88	02	Lower Little Five	19	11	1.95	1.43	354	49
88	03	Mid - Upper Little Five	51	36	1.92	1.80	961	269
89		**Rattlesnake Creek**						
89	07	Little Claire Lake	17	11	2.47	1.25	376	24
90		**Hockett Meadow**						
90	01	Atwell - Hockett Trail	24	14	2.21	1.80	479	43
90	03	Horse Creek Crossing	20	11	2.70	1.88	771	87
90	06	Hockett Meadow	22	18	2.36	2.40	662	144
90	09	Sand Meadow	5	1	1.20	0.00	10	2
90	14	Quinn R.S. - Soda Creek	6	3	1.50	1.33	40	8

* Some portions of these management areas may not have been inventoried in the 1970s.

Appendix 6: Change in campsite impact by subzone, ordered beginning with those with the greatest proportional decrease in aggregate impact

The following subzones contain areas within them that were surveyed in 2006-2007 but not in the late 1970s: 45-1 (Barrett Lakes), 46-6 (Bench Lake), 47-1 (Amphitheater Lake), 64-2 (Stream to Bullfrog), 75-3 (Moose Lake), 75-4 (Tamarack Lake), 80-3 (Shepherd Pass Lake), and 83-1 (Guitar Lake). As a result, estimates of change in these subzones are somewhat misleading. The improvement in conditions that occurred in all of these subzones other than 80-3 (Shepherd Pass Lake) is underestimated and the deterioration in conditions that occurred in the 80-3 (Shepherd Pass Lake) subzone is overestimated.

Zone	Subzone	Zone/Subzone	Percent Change in Weighted Value	Weighted Value per Campable Mile, 1976-1981	Weighted Value per Campable Mile, 2006-2007	Weighted Value per hectare, 1976-1981	Weighted Value per hectare, 2006-2007
33	06	South High Lakes	-100%	105	0	5	0
63	01	Charlotte/Gardiner Trail	-100%	865	0	10	0
61	03	Upper 60 Lakes	-97%	442	13	399	12
54	05	South Granite Basin	-96%	182	7	20	1
39	06	Grouse Meadow	-96%	2700	107	98	4
62	01	Dollar Lake	-95%	1028	50	239	12
34	02	McGee Lakes	-94%	448	28	92	6
89	07	Little Claire Lake	-94%	1253	80	247	16
83	04	Upper Whitney Creek	-94%	622	40	385	25
64	03	Lower Kearsarge Lake	-93%	2348	160	3238	221
54	07	Lower Tent Meadow	-93%	1840	128	66	5
54	02	Granite Basin Trail	-93%	474	34	126	10
62	03	Rae Lake 3	-93%	1079	78	881	63
83	06	Timberline Lake	-93%	1670	120	229	16
63	03	Charlotte Lake	-92%	2586	186	452	32
72	07	West Fork Ferguson Creek	-92%	25	2	9	1
64	05	Kearsarge Lake 3	-92%	1956	156	2204	176
62	07	Dragon Lake	-92%	617	50	36	3
83	05	Crabtree R.S.	-91%	1081	92	1545	131
54	01	Granite Lake	-91%	541	47	267	23
64	01	High Trail	-91%	1185	105	72	6
90	01	Atwell - Hockett Trail	-91%	5322	430	23	2
83	08	Upper Crabtree Meadow	-91%	361	33	468	42
33	02	Darwin Canyon	-91%	808	76	86	8
83	10	Crabtree Lakes	-90%	185	18	53	5
77	02	Alta Meadow	-90%	472	47	65	6
73	04	Ranger Lake	-90%	1475	147	268	27
33	03	Evolution Meadow	-90%	568	58	277	28
62	06	South Rae Lake 2	-90%	1415	147	618	64
62	04	North Rae Lake 2	-89%	333	36	189	20
70	03	Cement Table	-89%	435	47	145	16
90	03	Horse Creek Crossing	-89%	2570	290	517	58
39	03	Little Pete Meadow	-89%	1797	203	146	16
86	05	Kern Ranger Station	-88%	236	28	90	10
88	01	Long Lake	-88%	443	53	75	9
58	02	Castle Domes Meadow	-88%	879	105	361	43
51	04	Tehipite Valley	-88%	802	98	19	2
39	07	JMT - Simpson Junction	-87%	3550	445	60	8

90

Zone	Subzone	Zone/Subzone	Percent Change in Weighted Value	Weighted Value per Campable Mile, 1976-1981	Weighted Value per Campable Mile, 2006-2007	Weighted Value per Campable Mile, 1976-1981	Weighted Value per Campable Mile, 2006-2007
84	04	Funston-Forgotten	-87%	114	15	3	0
38	02	Upper Blue Canyon	-86%	443	61	25	3
88	02	Lower Little Five	-86%	885	123	398	55
84	01	Guyot Creek	-86%	720	100	3	0
62	02	Arrowhead Lake	-86%	602	85	278	39
62	05	Sixty Lakes Pass Lake	-86%	490	70	84	12
85	03	Soldier Lake	-85%	1262	184	137	20
33	05	Colby Meadow	-85%	525	79	348	52
75	04	Tamarack Lake*	-84%	982	153	60	9
28	02	San Joaquin River	-84%	550	87	81	13
46	07	Lake Marjorie	-84%	300	48	51	8
64	06	Upper Kearsarge Lake	-84%	465	75	53	9
85	02	Upper Rock Creek	-84%	311	51	21	3
85	04	Middle Rock Creek	-83%	633	106	307	51
38	03	Lower Blue Canyon	-83%	1345	225	11	2
64	04	Kearsarge Lakes 1 and 2	-83%	1871	314	1741	292
39	08	Deer Meadow	-83%	1499	253	114	19
79	06	Lower Kern-Kaweah	-83%	553	93	15	2
61	01	Lower 60 Lakes	-83%	166	29	49	9
39	04	LeConte Ranger Station	-82%	4380	785	192	34
46	04	Taboose Pass	-82%	276	51	29	5
46	06	Bench Lake*	-81%	1541	286	101	19
66	02	Sphinx Creek	-81%	814	153	172	32
83	09	Lower Crabtree Meadow	-81%	501	94	32	6
55	01	Above Paradise Valley	-81%	368	72	73	14
83	02	Sand Meadow	-80%	17	3	2	0
90	14	Quinn R.S.-Soda Creek	-80%	200	40	3	1
63	2	Below Charlotte Lake	-79%	1080	225	117	24
28	01	Piute Creek Bridge	-79%	1305	277	1424	302
52	01	Kennedy Pass	-79%	92	20	28	6
65	05	JMT – N of Forester Pass	-79%	705	151	53	11
83	02	Sandy Meadow	-79%	89	19	19	4
46	02	JMT – S Fork Kings	-78%	236	51	98	21
90	06	Hockett Meadow	-78%	2207	480	73	16
33	04	McClure Meadow	-78%	825	183	505	112
75	01	Table Meadow	-77%	70	16	20	4
64	02	Stream to Bullfrog*	-77%	566	128	956	217
79	04	Upper Kern Kaweah	-76%	57	14	11	3

Zone	Subzone	Zone/Subzone	Percent Change in Weighted Value	Weighted Value per Campable Mile, 1976-1981	Weighted Value per Campable Mile, 2006-2007	Weighted Value per Campable Mile, 1976-1981	Weighted Value per Campable Mile, 2006-2007
70	08	Colby Lake	-76%	193	47	16	4
80	04	Below Lake South America	-74%	440	112	26	7
39	02	Big Pete Meadow	-74%	1665	433	36	9
74	04	Silliman Lake	-74%	134	35	7	2
70	01	Big Brewer Lake	-74%	171	45	27	7
53	04	East Glacier Lakes	-73%	225	62	23	6
39	01	Upper LeConte	-72%	549	152	41	11
88	03	Mid - Upper Little Five	-72%	686	192	179	50
85	01	Miter Basin – Sky Blue	-72%	192	54	15	4
87	02	Lower - Mid Big Arroyo	-72%	107	30	22	6
79	01	Milestone Creek	-71%	313	90	8	2
81	04	Upper Wallace Creek	-70%	354	106	60	18
74	03	Cahoon Gap	-69%	81	26	78	24
84	02	Lower Rock Creek	-67%	382	124	54	18
34	01	Evolution Lake	-67%	417	138	156	51
63	04	Vidette to Bullfrog	-67%	930	310	152	51
39	05	Ladder/Rambaud	-65%	195	68	5	2
80	07	Lakes above Tyndall	-64%	2235	810	229	83
65	04	Center Basin	-64%	420	153	40	15
81	01	Wright Lakes	-63%	465	170	20	7
65	03	JMT – below Center B	-61%	1439	557	185	72
86	03	Rattlesnake Crossing	-61%	540	210	49	19
83	03	Timberline to Guitar	-60%	177	70	27	11
86	02	Upper Funston	-55%	748	340	64	29
72	01	Sugarloaf Valley	52%	101	49	40	19
79	03	Milestone Bowl	-52%	17	8	5	2
83	01	Guitar Lake*	-50%	2808	1398	175	87
45	01	Barrett Lakes*	-47%	129	68	11	6
87	01	Upper Big Arroyo	-47%	114	61	30	16
47	04	Kid Lakes	-45%	93	51	1	1
77	01	Panther Gap – Alta	-41%	773	453	35	21
75	03	Moose Lake*	-26%	196	144	13	10
86	01	Kern Hot Springs	-22%	1495	1170	183	144
47	01	Amphitheater Lake*	-19%	290	235	3	2
86	04	Funston Meadow	-13%	147	129	15	13
80	08	Bighorn Plateau	-11%	45	40	1	1
28	07	Martha Lake	-9%	59	54	6	5
33	01	Lake 11110	-4%	34	33	1	1

92

Zone	Subzone	Zone/Subzone	Percent Change in Weighted Value	Weighted Value per Campable Mile, 1976-1981	Weighted Value per Campable Mile, 2006-2007	Weighted Value per Campable Mile, 1976-1981	Weighted Value per Campable Mile, 2006-2007
84	03	Siberian Pass Trail	10%	62	68	2	2
83	07	Hitchcock Lakes	19%	45	53	9	11
79	02	Upper Kern	44%	80	115	9	13
79	07	Nine Lakes Basin	46%	240	350	6	8
80	01	Lakes S of Forester Pass	65%	325	535	6	10
80	03	Shepherd Pass Lake*	352%	210	950	9	41

* Some portions of these management areas may not have been inventoried in the 1970s.

Appendix 7: Campsite Monitoring Recommendations and Procedures

Monitoring Recommendations

The first recommendation for an ongoing monitoring program is that the data collected on restoration sites should be the same as the data collected on campsites. This includes condition class ratings. Restoration sites could be distinguished by adding two additional options to the site history field. Currently site history options are: normal use, rehabilitated and used and new site. The additional categories could be humanly restored and unused and naturally restored and unused. This would allow for more comparability with the initial campsite inventory and provide more options for analysis.

The second recommendation is that all impact parameters be recorded for all sites, rather than for just a sample of sites. There also might be value in altering some of the procedures for assessing campsite condition. The following difficulties with the existing system were noted by field data collectors:

Vegetation density with regard to surroundings can be accurately rated by a non-botanist, but how to rate vegetation composition (in relation to surroundings) is usually far less obvious.

Litter and duff ratings vary greatly with the season of visit.

Total campsite size can be rated quite differently by different observers.

Campsite development categories were developed based on conditions in the 1970s. They do not apply well to the less-developed conditions that exist today.

Mutilations to trees are not easy to quantify accurately.

The most troublesome element was barren core.

Similar concerns have been reported elsewhere. The Inyo National Forest adopted the Sequoia-Kings Canyon protocol, but dropped the vegetation composition and litter and duff elements because they were so problematic. No other recreation areas we are aware of monitor change in vegetation composition because it requires botanical knowledge and, except where impact is minor, little vegetation remains anyway. Several studies have found that ratings for tree mutilations, social trails, and loss of litter and duff exposing mineral soil are particularly imprecise (Cole 1989, Williams and Marion 1995). Total campsite size estimates, particularly where it is given a class rating rather than a measurement (such as square feet or meters), tend to be much more precise.

Unavoidably, management must make a trade-off between the time and resources that must be invested in campsite monitoring and value of the information that is collected. Moreover, for any given level of investment, there is a trade-off between the quantity and precision of information. The campsite monitoring protocols used in this study at Sequoia and Kings Canyon National Parks can be characterized as requiring a low investment (usually only a minute or two spent at each campsite), providing a large quantity of information (8 impact parameters) of relatively low precision. Where they can be afforded, it is hard to argue against investing more resources in monitoring procedures that provide large quantities of high quality information. Farrell and Marion (1998), and Cole et al. (2008) for example, have monitored campsites using relatively precise techniques that require from 30 minutes to more than an hour per campsite.

However, when there are several thousand campsites, as there are in Sequoia and Kings Canyon National Parks, such an investment may be prohibitively expensive. At the low investment extreme, the Forest Service has developed what they refer to as the minimum protocol—the least costly set of procedures that can provide meaningful monitoring data on which to build a campsite management program. This protocol involves doing a complete census of campsites, while collecting three bits of information on campsite condition, none of which should require more than the time it takes to collect GPS locational information. These three impact parameters (groundcover disturbance, tree damage and area of disturbance) were selected because they are important long-lasting types of impact that often do not covary. That is, certain campsites are intensely disturbed but small, while others might be large but less-intensely disturbed and regardless of disturbance intensity or extent, trees may be damaged or not. These protocols (described below)—perhaps in modified format—might be worth considering for future monitoring efforts in Sequoia and Kings Canyon National Parks.

Procedures for Inventorying Campsites

Identify all the locations where campsites are likely to be located on a map and develop a plan to visit all these places. This would include all trail corridors as well as off-trail routes and destinations that receive regular use. The inventory can be conducted in a single field season or it can be done over several seasons. For example, a large wilderness might plan to inventory 1/5 of their area every year repeatedly, accomplishing a complete reinventory every 5 years.

Areas that are searched for campsites need to be documented so it is clear when new campsites are found whether it is a new campsite or perhaps an old campsite in a place that has never been searched before. Every place that has been clearly impacted by camping should be inventoried as a campsite, even if the site is to be restored. Where campfires are allowed, campfire remains (e.g. scattered charcoal) provide the most reliable indication of campsite impact on very lightly-impacted campsites. Where campfires are not allowed, other criteria will have to be developed for identifying lightly-impacted campsites. At each inventoried campsite, use a GPS to obtain site coordinates. These procedures are identical to those already used at Sequoia and Kings Canyon National Parks.

Procedures for Assessing Campsite Condition

Independently assess (1) groundcover disturbance of the main campsite, (2) impact to standing trees and roots, and (3) size of disturbed area (including satellite tent pads and stock-holding areas). Each of these three parameters should be separately assessed. They are combined in a single impact index but the individual ratings will be kept separate as well.

Record disturbance to the groundcover of the central portion of the campsite (disregarding satellite disturbed areas) as one of the following classes. Select a midpoint when the condition is close to the boundary between classes.

1. Ground vegetation flattened but not permanently injured. Minimal physical change except for possibly a simple rock fireplace.

2. Ground vegetation worn away around fireplace or center of activity.

3. Ground vegetation lost on most of the site, but humus and litter still present in all but a few areas.

4. Bare mineral soil widespread over most of the campsite.

Note that this rating integrates the vegetation density, litter and duff and barren core parameters of the current protocol.

As a general rule of thumb, if bare area (without vegetation) is virtually absent, assign a rating of 1. If bare area is obvious at the center of the site, extending out somewhat from a fire ring, but a single 2-person tent would extend onto portions of the site that are still vegetated (i.e. the bare area cannot accommodate both a fire ring and a single tent), assign the site a rating of 2. If the central bare area is large enough to accommodate a fire ring, as well as two 2-person tents, assign a rating of 3 (if most of the bare area still retains a humus/litter cover) or a rating of 4 (if the humus/litter cover is gone from most of the site). A site with enough bare area to accommodate a fire ring and one adjacent 2-person tent would be given a rating of 2.5.

Record tree damage as one of the following classes, depending on the number of trees that have been severely damaged. Assess damage off-site as well as on-site, particularly in stock-holding areas associated with the campsite. Include any trees judged to have been damaged as a result of camping activities at the site being monitored. Severely damaged trees are those that (1) have been felled and are at least 10 cm (4 inches) in diameter where felled (if trees have multiple stems, consider the tree felled if any stem at least 10 cm (4 inches) in diameter has been cut off); (2) have scarring that exceeds 1000 cm^2 (1 ft^2) in total area or (3) have highly exposed roots (more than 1 m (3 feet) of root sticks out at least 2.5 cm (1 inch) above the ground surface). Select a midpoint when the condition is close to the boundary between classes.

0. No more than 3 severely damaged trees.

1. 4 to 10 severely damaged trees.

2. More than 10 severely damaged trees.

Campsites without trees should be given a rating of 0 for this parameter. This procedure allows for horse-holding areas to be included and should be easier to apply than current procedures because it is based on a count of trees rather than individual mutilations. Given relatively low levels of tree damage on campsites, it may be worthwhile having more stringent criteria, such as class 1 starting when there are either 1 or 2 severely damaged trees.

Record disturbed area as one of the following classes, depending on the size of the area disturbed by camping activities, including the main campsite, satellite tent pads and areas where horses are confined. In most situations, disturbed places are distinguished by obvious vegetation loss (either complete lack of vegetation or sparse vegetation resulting from trampling). Places where vegetation has been flattened but is likely to recover in the short-term should **not** be included in the disturbed area. Where vegetation is naturally absent, it may be necessary to identify disturbed places on the basis of flattening of soil or litter on the forest floor (see special situation 1 below). When there are multiple separate disturbed parts of the campsite, do NOT include undisturbed areas in between. For example, if there is a main campsite, two tent pads and a stock-holding area, assess the size of each of the four areas separately and then sum them. Social trails between separate disturbed areas can be ignored. Select a midpoint when the condition is close to the boundary between classes.

0. No more than 25 m^2 (0-250 ft^2).

1. 26 to 100 m^2 (251 - 1000 ft^2).

2. More than 100 m^2 (more than 1000 ft^2).

Using this protocol, assign the campsite an overall impact rating between 1 and 8. This is the sum of the groundcover disturbance rating (1-4), the tree damage rating (0-2) and the disturbed area rating (0-2).

Special Situations

On sites without organic soil horizons and/or much perennial vegetation (for example, sites on rock or sites in the dense shade where understory vegetation is absent), the **groundcover** class definitions must be adapted. It would be good to note whether standard or adapted groundcover classes were used. In ecosystem types with a poorly developed organic soil horizon, use the level of soil compaction to differentiate between class 3 and class 4 campsites.

Where there is sparse but regularly-distributed perennial vegetation, use the size of the central area from which all perennial vegetation has been eliminated (regardless of the annual vegetation) to differentiate between class 2 and class 3. Where there is little perennial vegetation, use the size of the central area that has experienced long-term flattening of the soil surface to differentiate between class 2 and class 3. This might involve flattening/abrasion of forest litter in dense shade. Conversely, a campsite entirely confined to vegetation-less sand or a rocky ledge would always get a rating of 1 because there is no long-term flattening of the soil.

Ratings for sites in ecosystem types that have perennial vegetation but lack organic horizons would be as follows:

1. Evidence of camping but minimal physical change except for possibly a simple rock fireplace.

2. Perennial vegetation gone and soil surface flattened (for the long-term) around fireplace or center of activity.

3. Perennial vegetation gone and soil surface flattened (for the long-term) on most of the site, but exposed mineral soil not highly compacted except in a few areas.

4. Mineral soil exposed and highly compacted (to a cement-like state) over most of the campsite.

Ratings for sites in ecosystem types that lack both perennial vegetation and organic horizons would be as follows:

1. Evidence of camping but minimal physical change except for possibly a simple rock fireplace.

2. Soil surface flattened (for the long-term) around fireplace or center of activity.

3. Soil surface flattened (for the long-term) on most of the site, but exposed mineral soil not highly compacted except in a few areas.

4. Mineral soil exposed and highly compacted (to a cement-like state) over most of the campsite.

This minimum protocol has been criticized because it provides relatively little information (e.g. it provides no information on social trails, campsite development or size of barren core) and it lacks a high degree of quantification. More parameters could be added to the ratings. However, this would not necessarily change overall ratings much as social trailing and size of barren core generally should co-vary with the groundcover disturbance rating. Quantitative measures have the advantage of being more sensitive than an ordinal rating. Knowing the campsite area changed from 300 ft^2 to 3000 ft^2 is much more informative than knowing that its disturbed area rating changed from 1 to 2. The problem is that estimates of campsite area are so imprecise (unless one spends 30 minutes or more on the site), that quantitative estimates can be highly misleading.

Perhaps the ideal approach would be to complete a census of sites using rapid procedures, such as the minimum protocol or the original procedures used at Sequoia and Kings Canyon National Parks and then supplement this with more precise and detailed measures on a sample of sites, as was done in Grand Canyon National Park (Cole et al. 2008).

Conclusion

There is nothing wrong with current procedures if an inventory of the entire wilderness is completed, if such data are collected more frequently than every 30 years, if condition information is collected for restoration sites and all parameters are recorded for all campsites. However, some revision of current procedures, perhaps an adaptation of the minimum protocol, is worth considering. If protocols are changed, it would be advisable to apply both old and new protocols the first time the shift is made. This would not add much time, as each protocol requires no more than about a minute per site.

Literature Cited

Cole, D. N., P. Foti and M. Brown. 2008. Twenty years of change on campsites in the backcountry of Grand Canyon National Park. Environmental Management 41: 959-970.

Appendix 8: Sample Maps of Campsites

In this appendix we show maps from two subzones. We could not include maps from all subzones surveyed as they were too numerous for this publication and made the file size too large. Three maps are provided for each subzone. One map shows the sites present during the 2006-2007 survey. Actively-used campsites are classified according to their campsite condition, between 1 and 4. Sites impacted by camping, but no longer being used, are shown as restoration sites. A second map, using the same base map, shows the locations of campsites present during the initial survey in the late 1970s. The third map is a reproduction of maps produced in the late 1970s, by placing a dot on a topographic map, with the size of the dot reflective of the site's condition class rating. In addition to showing campsite condition class, these maps also show topography and the trail system and hydrography at that time period.

One should use caution when comparing the precise campsite locations for the two time periods. On the 2006-2007 map, the campsite locations should be highly accurate because they were located using GPS technology; however, the trails and hydrography are not always as accurately located. So the location of campsites relative to trails and hydrography may not always be accurate. On the late 1970s "dot" map, campsites were located based on their proximity to trails and hydrography. Because, those were sometimes inaccurate and subject to change, campsite locations may be inaccurate. This explains why on some maps, a few campsites appear to be in the lake. Finally, there may be slight discrepancies between the number of sites on these maps and the numbers presented in Appendices 1 and 5. This usually results from field surveyors assigning a site close to the boundary between subzones to a subzone other than the subzone drawn on the maps.

Guitar Lake (83-01): 1978

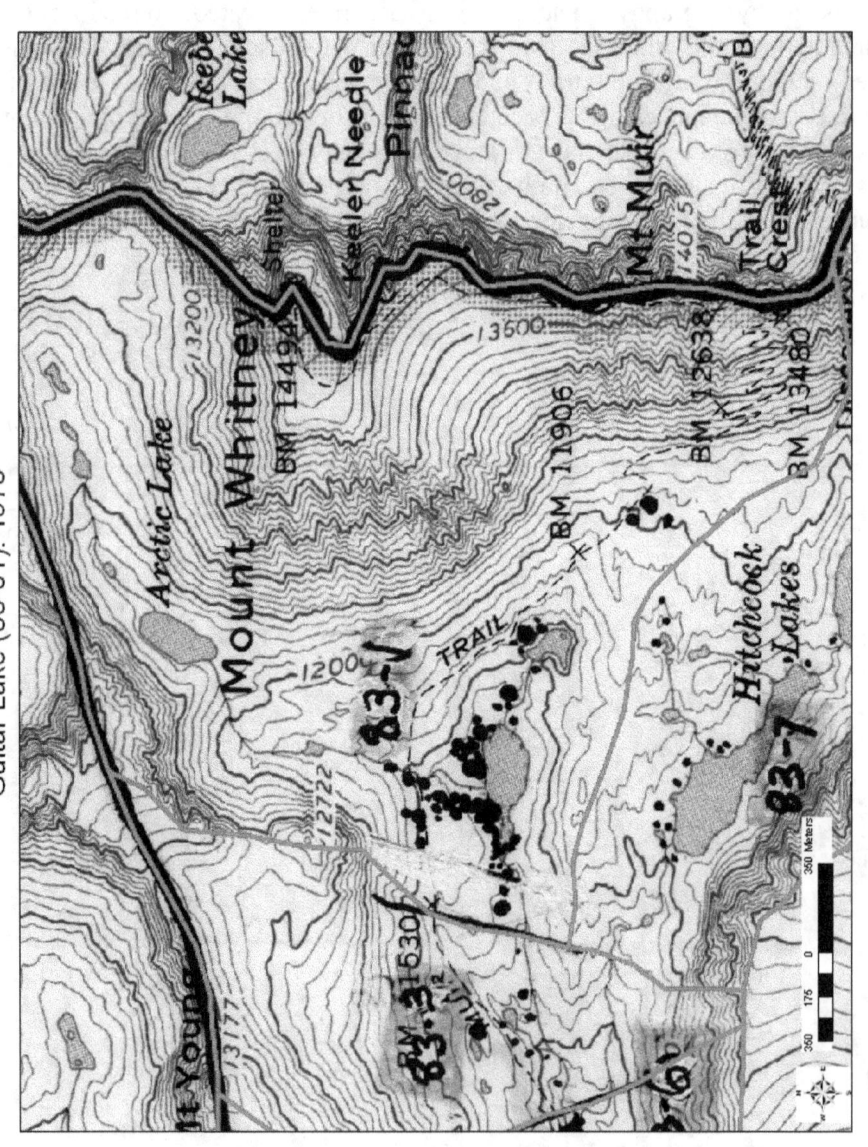

Figure 8-1a. Digitized original map from 1978 survey of campsites in the Guitar Lake area of Sequoia National Park. Black dots were hand-drawn to indicate campsite location and dots were scaled to represent campsite condition class rating. These campsite locations are approximate, as Global Positioning Devices were not available at the time of the original survey.

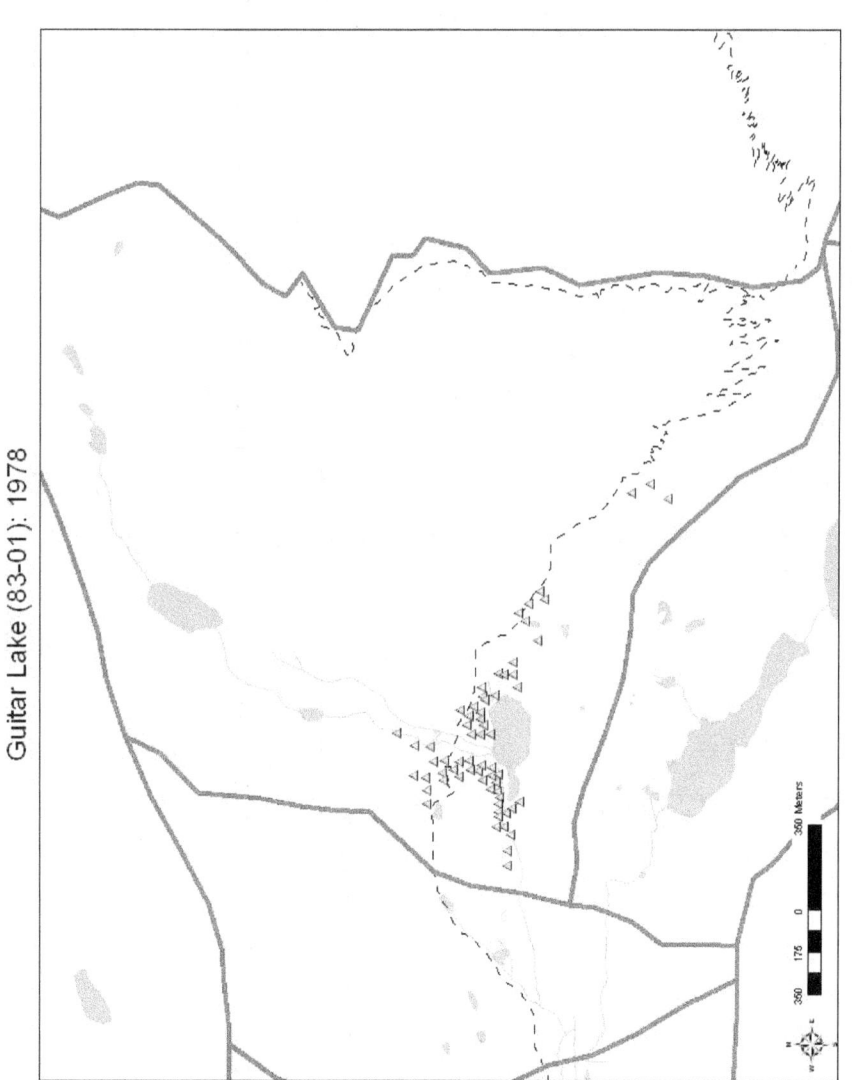

Figure 8-1b. Schematic map of Guitar Lake area in Sequoia National Park showing the campsites present during the 1978 survey.

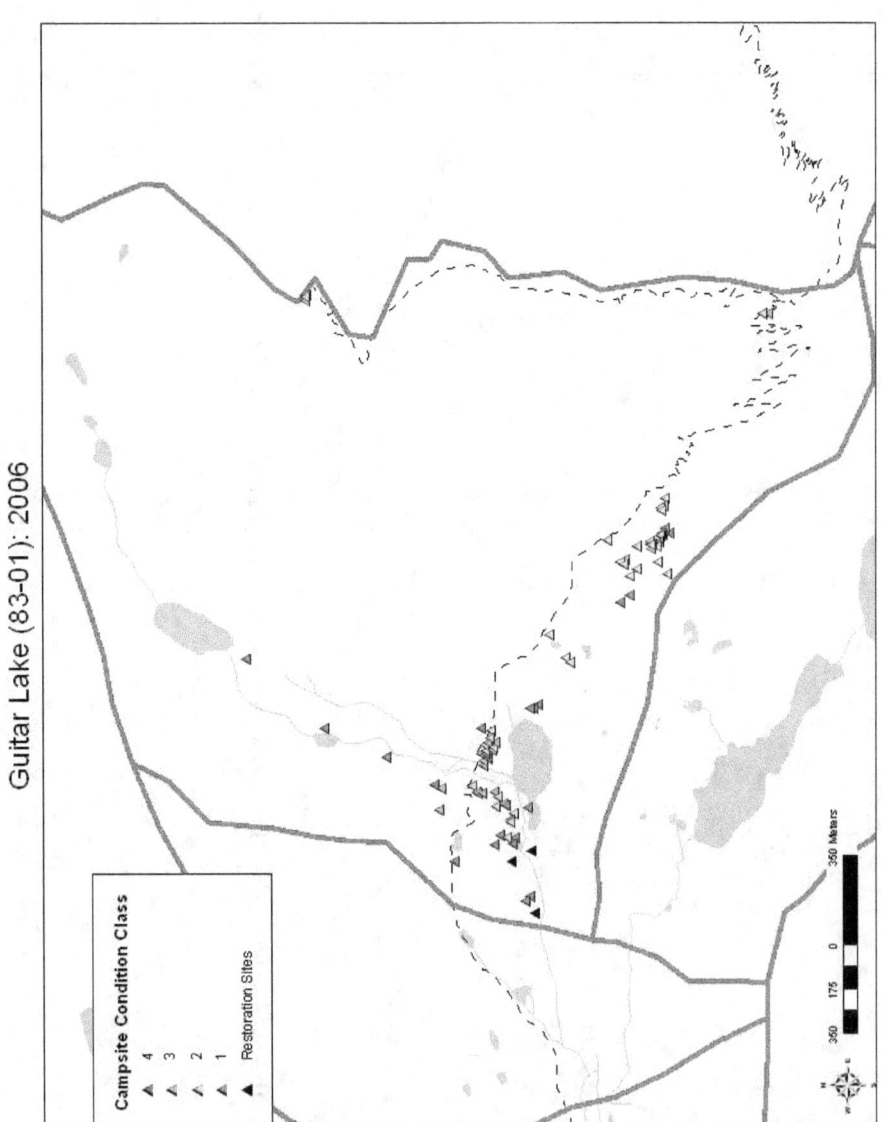

Guitar Lake (83-01): 2006

Campsite Condition Class
△ 4
△ 3
△ 2
△ 1
▲ Restoration Sites

350 175 0 350 Meters

Figure 8-1c. Schematic map of Guitar Lake area in Sequoia National Park showing the campsites present during the 2006 re-survey and the site condition classes.

Granite Lake (54-01): 1979

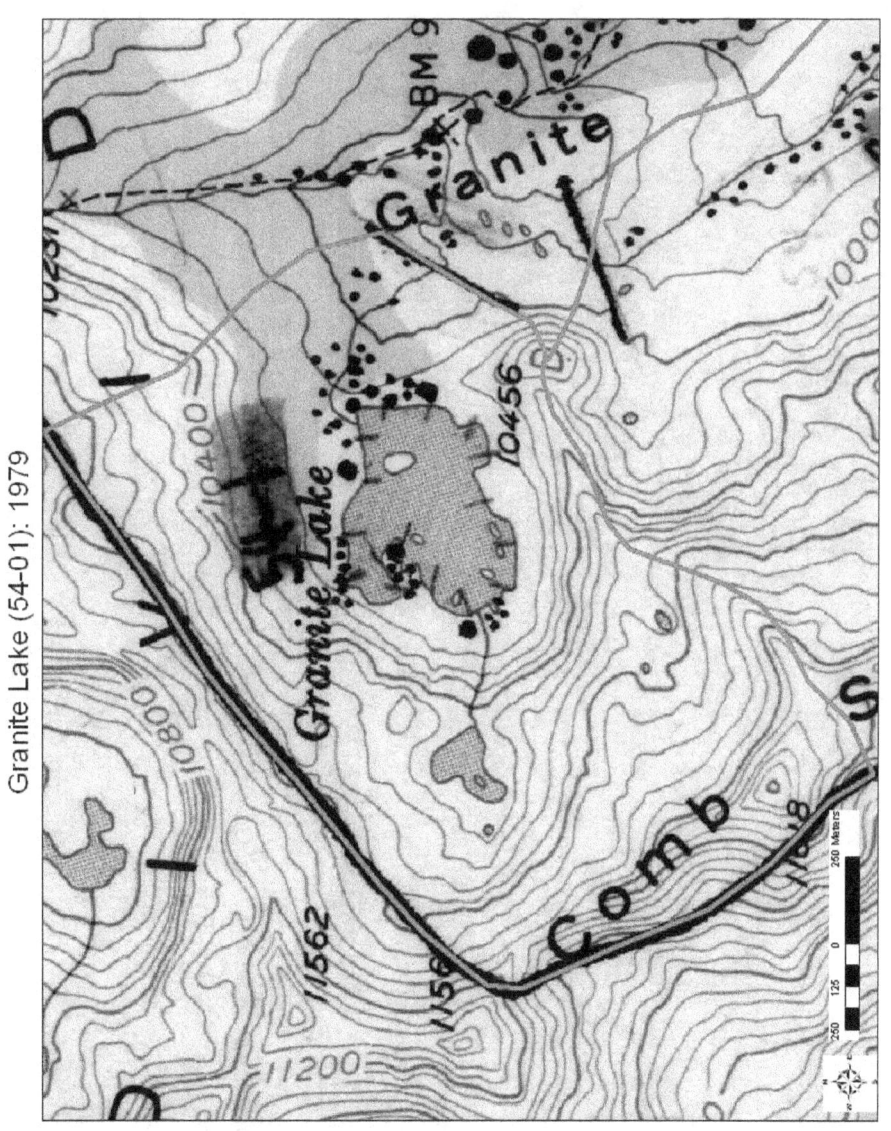

Figure 8-2a. Digitized original map from 1979 survey of campsites in the Granite Lake area of Kings Canyon National Park. Black dots were hand-drawn to indicate campsite location and dots were scaled to represent campsite condition class rating. These campsite locations are approximate, as Global Positioning Devices were not available at the time of the original survey.

Granite Lake (54-01): 1979

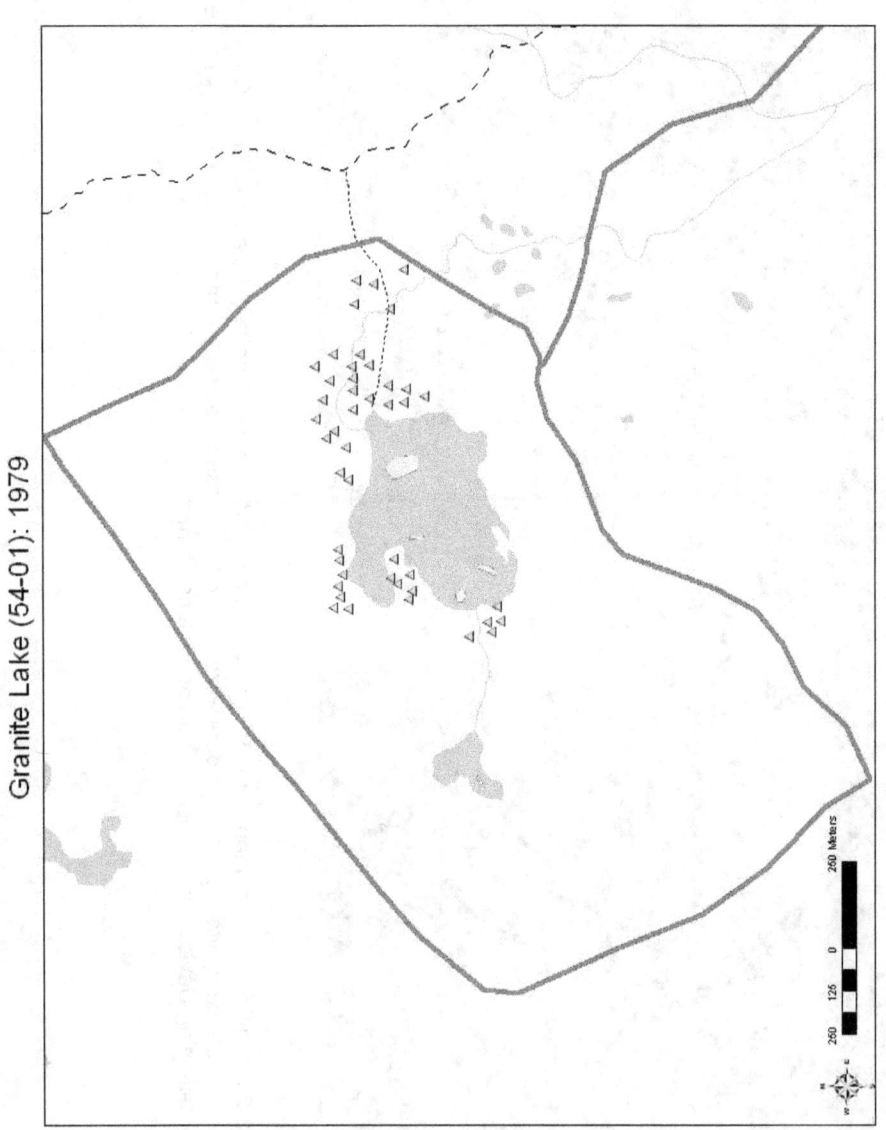

250 125 0   250 Meters

Figure 8-2b. Schematic map of Granite Lake area in Kings Canyon National Park showing the campsites present during the 1979 survey.

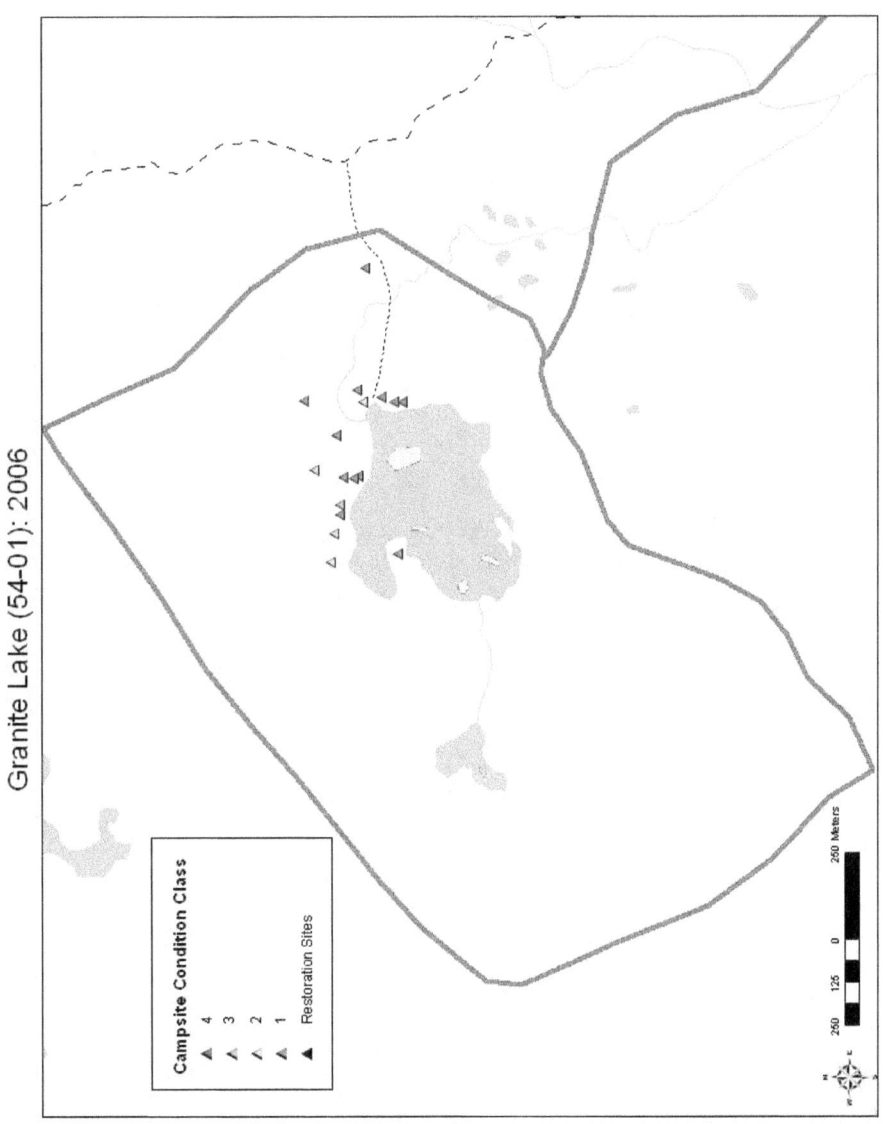

Figure 8-2c. Schematic map of Granite Lake area in Kings Canyon National Park showing the campsites present during the 2006 re-survey and the site condition classes.

107

NPS 102/119561, January 2013

www.ingramcontent.com/pod-product-compliance
Lightning Source LLC
Chambersburg PA
CBHW081108290526

45795CB00006B/2040